The American History Series

SERIES EDITORS
John Hope Franklin, *Duke University*
Abraham S. Eisenstadt, *Brooklyn College*

Arthur S. Link
Princeton University
GENERAL EDITOR FOR HISTORY

C. S. Griffin
THE UNIVERSITY OF KANSAS

The Ferment
of Reform

1830–1860

HARLAN DAVIDSON, INC.
ARLINGTON HEIGHTS, ILLINOIS 60004

ISBN: 0-88295-738-4
(Formerly 0-690-29568-5)

Library of Congress Card Number: 67-13380

THIS BOOK IS DEDICATED TO MELVIN L. WILSON
Historian of reform, yet no reformer he

Cover design: Roger Eggers
Cover illustration: The Bettman Archive

Manufactured in the United States of America
95 94 93 92 91 MA   11 12 13 14 16

EDITORS' FOREWORD

Every generation writes its own history, for the reason that it sees the past in the foreshortened perspective of its own experience. This has certainly been true of the writing of American history. The practical aim of our historiography is to offer us a more certain sense of where we are going by helping us understand the road we took in getting where we are. If the substance and nature of our historical writing is changing, it is precisely because our own generation is redefining its direction, much as the generations that preceded us redefined theirs. We are seeking a newer direction, because we are facing new problems, changing our values and premises, and shaping new institutions to meet new needs. Thus, the vitality of the present inspires the vitality of our writing about our past. Today's scholars are hard at work reconsidering every major field of our history: its politics, diplomacy, economy, society, mores, values, sexuality, and status, ethnic, and race relations. No less significantly, our scholars are using newer modes of investigation to probe the ever-expanding domain of the American past.

Our aim, in this American History Series, is to offer the reader a survey of what scholars are saying about the central themes and issues of American history. To present these themes and issues, we have invited scholars who have made notable contributions to the respective fields in which they are writing. Each volume offers the reader a sufficient factual and narrative account for perceiving the larger dimensions of its particular subject. Addressing their respective themes, our authors have undertaken, moreover, to present the conclusions derived by the principal writers on these themes. Beyond that, the authors present their own conclusions about those aspects of their respective subjects that have been matters of difference and controversy. In effect, they have written not only about where the subject stands in today's historiography but also about where they stand on their subject. Each volume closes with an extensive critical essay on the writings of the major authorities on its particular theme.

The books in this series are designed for use in both basic and advanced courses in American history. Such a series has a particular utility in times such as these, when the traditional format of our American history courses is being altered to accommodate a greater diversity of texts and reading materials. The series offers a number of distinct advantages. It extends and deepens the dimensions of course work in American history. In proceeding beyond the confines of the traditional textbook, it makes clear that the study of our past is, more than the student might otherwise infer, at once complex, sophisticated, and profound. It presents American history as a subject of continuing vitality and fresh investigation. The work of experts in their respective fields, it opens up to the student the rich findings of historical inquiry. It invites the student to join, in major fields of research, the many groups of scholars who are pondering anew the central themes and problems of our past. It challenges the student to participate actively in exploring American history and to collaborate in the creative and rigorous adventure of seeking out its wider reaches.

John Hope Franklin

Abraham S. Eisenstadt

CONTENTS

ACKNOWLEDGMENTS: The only comprehensive account of historians' ideas about antebellum reform is Melvin L. Wilson's excellent analysis, *Reform as Puzzle: Historians View Ante-Bellum Reform* (Unpublished M.A. thesis, University of Kansas, 1966). I have learned much from it; and, with Mr. Wilson's permission, I have frequently used his discoveries. He is not, however, responsible for my interpretations. Mr. Kenneth L. Smock rendered valuable aid as my research assistant.

ONE

The Idea of Reform

"In the history of the world," Ralph Waldo Emerson wrote in 1841, "the doctrine of Reform had never such scope as at the present hour." The great reformers of the past, he said, "Lutherans, Herrnhutters, Jesuits, Monks, Quakers, Knox, Wesley, Swedenborg, Bentham, in their accusations of society, all respected something,—church or state, literature or history, domestic usages, the market town, the dinner table, coined money. But now all these and all things else hear the trumpet, and must rush to judgment,—Christianity, the laws, commerce, schools, the farm, the laboratory;

I

and not a kingdom, town, statute, rite, calling, man, or woman, but is threatened by the new spirit." What Emerson called the "demon of reform" was abroad in the land, and no one was proof against the demon's wiles.

If there was a certain poetic hyperbole in Emerson's words, he had nevertheless caught very neatly one of the dominant characteristics of the antebellum United States. During the years from 1830 to 1860 a host of reformers in a variety of reform movements together examined and attacked every American institution, every idea, every conceivable sin, evil, or burden of suffering. Against slavery stood thousands of abolitionists; against the horrors of war stood a small army of pacifists; against liquor drinking, drunkenness, and the neighborhood saloon stood cadres of prohibitionists striving to make cold water the national beverage. While some reformers worked to wipe out prostitution, saving the whores from sin and shame and their clients from temptation, other reformers—good Protestants, they—labored in various ways to destroy Roman Catholicism. Still other reformers tried to redeem criminals by changing the prison environment, to help the mentally incompetent and the physically disabled toward happier lives, to provide public schools and colleges to educate the nation's children and lyceums to inform adults. Although most Americans continued to believe that traditional political and economic institutions best promoted the general welfare, many of their fellow citizens argued that communitarian or socialistic societies promised more, and a few men claimed that all coercive institutions were evil. Most Americans continued to accept one or another of the orthodox Protestant creeds, and there were numberless reformers seeking to bring the entire nation to Christ. But hard beside them other religious zealots created new cults and sects to offer men better ways toward a proper relation with that Spirit, or those spirits, which lay beyond space and time. The yeasty ferment of reform buoyed up Americans who would make women the political and social equals of men—hell had no fury like a women's-righter scorned; who would drastically change the people's dietary habits and modes of dress; who hewed away at the ancient institution of monogamy, letting lovers fall where they might.

Most reform movements had societies to spread their gospels. A few reformers, like Henry David Thoreau, might go it alone, but most enthusiasts knew that in union there was both moral and financial strength. The societies varied greatly in size and scope. On the one hand there were great national groups such as the American Bible Society, an interdenominational organization designed to save every soul in the land by putting a Bible in every home, or the American Anti-Slavery Society whose objective was to end Negro bondage. On the other hand there were multitudes of local reform societies in the nation's cities and hamlets. "Matters have come to such a pass," one sour observer said in 1838, "that a peaceable man can hardly venture to eat or drink, or to go to bed or to get up, to correct his children or to kiss his wife, without obtaining the permission and direction of some . . . society." Occasionally there appeared groups whose vision was grandly comprehensive. Thus in 1840 a motley group of radicals gathered in Boston calling themselves the Friends of Universal Reform. Thus did Amos Bronson Alcott, a transcendentalist of an extreme type, ask—and get—idealistic New Englanders to join a Club for the Study and Diffusion of Ideas and Tendencies Proper to the Nineteenth Century.

So great was the ferment of reform in the pre-Civil War United States that to understand it, to grasp the motives of the reformers, the nature of their work, their successes and failures, is to understand much about the American nation as a whole. To be sure, there was more to antebellum history than reform. At the same time that the reformers were trying to change men's ideas and actions, other Americans were holding fast to traditional concepts and ways of doing things. Even as the reformers were battering the walls of unrighteousness, both they and other men were taming wild nature for human use, expanding the nation's boundaries and settled areas at the expense of Indians and Mexicans, adapting its political institutions and political parties to the needs of a restless and growing people, wrestling with the thousand and one problems inherent in the pursuit of happiness. Yet historians have believed that the myriad of reforms and reformers offer a meaning for much of the whirl and confusion and change that was America in the antebellum years. They offer as well, some historians have claimed, valuable insights into the difficulties the Americans encountered when they tried to give concrete meaning to their cherished ideals—so often voiced, so little understood—of democracy and freedom.

Unfortunately, however, historians have not agreed about either the meaning of reform or the insights it offered. A century after the ferment of reform merged with the larger ferment of civil war, there was still considerable perplexity surrounding the reformers and their efforts. The question that generated most of the disagreement and confusion was whether the reformers' work expressed ideas that were intrinsically good. A large majority of historians believed it did. In the majority view, the reformers as a group manifested ideas that were morally right, and upon which the American nation itself was founded: the principles of Christianity, the ideas of equality and natural rights set forth in the Declaration of Independence and cherished—albeit in new ways —by nineteenth-century democrats, the inevitability of progress in America. Antebellum reform, the majority of historians claimed, was evidence of the pervasive American conviction that men in a new land and a new era were at last free to shape the future to maximize their happiness. In reform allegedly lay a heightened sense of the meaning of the American democratic experiment itself.

Other historians were not so sure. A minority was not convinced that the reform movements were merely the antebellum American virtues in action. After all, they suggested, both good and evil might lie only in the eye of the beholder. The meaning of Christianity or democracy or the Declaration of Independence might depend upon the interpreter, and one man's progress might well be another man's regress. If freedom, for example, could be defined as the right of each man to seek happiness in his own way as long as he did not disturb the social order, did the prohibition movement promote freedom or restrict it? When liquor drinkers fought the prohibitionists in the name of freedom, of a decent respect for the rights of others, who had the better of the argument? To put the matter more broadly, all the reformers were demanding that men forsake old ways of thinking and doing in the name of eternal values. Yet many men saw virtue in the old ways and evil in the new. The minority of historians wondered how anyone could be sure where virtue actually lay.

Interestingly enough, the division among the historians about the nature and meaning of reform was much like the division that existed from 1830 to 1860 among the reformers and their contemporaries. While the ferment of reform was bubbling, there was no unanimity about its essence. What was most striking was that the reformers themselves were often at odds with each other. It was natural, after all, that slaveholders damn abolitionists as would-be tyrants seeking to deprive southerners of their freedom to own Negroes, natural that opponents of the women's rights crusade curse the leaders of that crusade as meddlesome fools attacking the relation between the sexes established by God Himself and His natural law. But within reform itself—begging, for a moment, the question of what reform was—the arguments were just as bitter. Like American society itself, antebellum reform was diverse, pluralistic; it tugged in different ways at different problems. A convert to the Mormonism of Joseph Smith, for example, might become a fervent evangelist of his new religion, and thereby a reformer. But as a Mormon reformer he suffered attack from hordes of orthodox Protestant religious reformers who saw Mormonism as one of the nation's more horrible evils. In 1857 an agent of the American Bible Society, a reform group if ever there was one, described the Mormons of Salt Lake City as drunkards and profane men, and portrayed the Mormon settlement as a "bedlam, brothel, sink of iniquity, Hades, and vortex of moral ruin." "Each individual," C. R. Van Emman claimed, "is a dupe, a serf, and an ignorant fool, each family is a house of prostitution and all liars, thieves, . . . libertines and fit subjects of any and all delusions." Similarly, there were temperance men who detested the women's rights movement, and labor union reformers who detested the temperance movement, and anti-Catholic reformers who detested labor unions and all their works. Ralph Waldo Emerson himself was one of the most comprehensive of antebellum reformers. As a transcendentalist he urged Americans toward new ways of knowing truth; toward spirituality instead of materialism; toward new ways of dwelling with nature, man, and God. Yet Emerson was extremely critical of what he considered the more ordinary reformer. "The Reforms have their high origin in an ideal justice," he wrote, again in 1841, "but they do not retain the purity of an idea." The reformers relied for success "not on love, not on a principle, but on men, on multitudes, on circumstances, on money. on party; that is, on fear, on wrath, and pride. . . . Those who are urging with most ardor what are called the greatest benefits of mankind, are narrow, self-pleasing, conceited men, and affect us as the insane do. They bite us, and we run mad also." Reform as the reformers practiced it was an annoying "buzz in the ear."

Yet Emerson was quick to admit that the theory of reform was as splendid as the practice was sordid. Most historians of the reform crusades have agreed with his description of reform itself, while rejecting his portrayal of the reformer. "The history of reform," Emerson said, "is always identical, it is the comparison of the idea with the fact. Our modes of living are not agreeable to our imagination," and men set out to make them so. Reform was an effort to "raise the life of man by putting it in harmony with his idea of the Beautiful and the Just." The origin of all reform, Emerson thought, was that "mysterious fountain of the moral senti-

ment in man, which, amidst the natural, ever contains the super-
natural for men"; the "spring and regulator" of all reform efforts
was the "conviction that there is an infinite worthiness in man,
which will appear at the call of worth, and that all particular reforms are the removing of some impediment."

So say most of the recent historians of the reform movements,
and so said most of their predecessors. The only book to attempt
to analyze the idea of reform throughout American history was
Arthur M. Schlesinger, Sr.'s brief study, *The American as Reformer* (Cambridge, 1951). Quoting Emerson frequently and en-
dorsing his comments, Schlesinger defined reform as a struggle for
"human betterment," as a "disposition to challenge vested injustice."
Reform meant "human gains," "social progress," and an "irref-
utable challenge to a repressive *status quo.*" By the mid-1960s,
surprisingly, there was still only one comprehensive treatment of
antebellum reform: Alice Felt Tyler's *Freedom's Ferment: Phases
of American Social History to 1860* (Minneapolis, 1944). Relying
less upon Emerson directly than did Schlesinger, Mrs. Tyler still
gave reform an Emersonian definition. Reform was a "desire to
perfect human institutions" which stemmed in great part from the
reformers' "belief in the worth of the individual"; a reformer was
one who had an "honest recognition of the worth of the individual
and of his right to develop his capacities." Russel B. Nye's *William
Lloyd Garrison and the Humanitarian Reformers* (Boston, 1955)
described reform as an attempt to alter every institution or tradition that "prevented realization of the individual's powers," and
the "complete development of the individual's capacities." Louis
Filler claimed in his *The Crusade against Slavery, 1830-1860*
(New York, 1960) that reform meant "respect for the rights of the
individual," that reform was a means for "magnifying the in-
dividual's qualities." According to Merton L. Dillon's *Elijah P.
Lovejoy, Abolitionist Editor* (Urbana, 1961) and Timothy L.
Smith's *Revivalism and Social Reform in Mid-Nineteenth-Century
America* (New York, 1957), reform meant to zealous Christians

God's "holy enterprise of sweeping away every man-made obstacle to pure religion, to virtue, and to freedom"; it was a crusade to "convert and civilize the globe, to purge human society of all its evils, and to usher in Christ's reign on earth."

Such general ideas about reform had been with the historical profession for years. In 1927, for example, Carl Russell Fish had argued in his *The Rise of the Common Man, 1830-1850* (New York) that the primary aim of reform was "to release the individual, to secure a real freedom," "to liberate the human soul." In 1936 Henry Steele Commager claimed in his biography of *Theodore Parker: Yankee Crusader* (Boston) that all the reformers were motivated by the idea of the infinite worthiness of man of which Emerson had spoken. "What had they in common—" Commager asked, "what but a belief in the perfectibility of man and in the doctrine of progress?" Commager said that Emerson spoke for all of them when he described and praised reform, and said that all reformers were transcendentalists. In a more recent work, *The Era of Reform, 1830-1860* (Princeton, 1960), Commager was still arguing, inelegantly, that Emerson was the "cow" from which all reformers "drew their milk."

The historians' approval of reform was obvious in their words. More important than their approval, however, was their general belief that the reformers as a group were giving a valid meaning to ideals that were the very foundations of the United States itself. Too long had Americans laughed at the peculiarities of antebellum eccentrics, Alice Felt Tyler wrote. Too long had people paid "amused attention" to such "fads and fancies" as phrenology, hydropathy, mesmerism, health and diet reforms, spiritualism, and free love. Both the American people and the American historians ought to give the reformers the respect they deserved. Reform, she said, was the manifestation of a general American hope that Christian virtue could be realized, combined with the "rationalism of Jefferson merged with the democracy of the frontier." Despite the changes wrought by the Civil War, by industrial capitalism, and by urbanization, the prewar crusaders had established the "fundamentals of the American faith and the American way of life." The reformers were "men to whom the life of the perfect Christ gave hope that their lives and their institutions might be perfected, men who saw no limits for the advancement of the individual or of the nation, men who were proud to fight in the cause of democracy and freedom." Most of Mrs. Tyler's successors agreed that antebellum reform expressed a quintessential Americanism. American Christianity and the ideas of the Declaration of Independence, Arthur M. Schlesinger, Sr., wrote in 1951, "sustained and refreshed the reform impulse." In an excellent study of *Fettered Freedom: Civil Liberties and the Slavery Controversy, 1830-1860* (East Lansing, 1949), Russel B. Nye saw reform as a "crusade to establish true democracy according to the Declaration of Independence, to break the power of the dominant aristocratic class, to perfect the social order, and to apply Christianity to American life." In 1961 Dwight L. Dumond published his *Antislavery: The Crusade for Freedom in America* (Ann Arbor), and the same idea appeared there. It was precisely because slavery was at odds with the dominant ideas of the day, expressed best by the reformers, that it vanished. "Need one wonder why an institution at war with the natural rights of man, the cardinal principles of the Christian faith, and the ideals of individual freedom and social progress was swept away?" Dumond asked. "The answer, of course, is an emphatic no!"

NAY SAYERS AND SKEPTICS

Such descriptions of antebellum reform and reformers both contain some truths of history and create some vexing problems for historians. In giving an essentially Emersonian definition of reform, the historians portrayed the reformers just as the reformers portrayed themselves. In July, 1848, for example, the world's first Women's Rights Convention gathered in Seneca Falls, New York, under the leadership of Lucretia Mott and Elizabeth Cady Stanton. To promote the cause of sexual equality, the oppressed females issued a Declaration of Sentiments modeled on the Declaration of Independence. "We hold these truths," the ladies said, "to be self-evident: that all men and women are created equal"; they went on to say that the Creator had endowed both sexes with the same "inalienable rights," among which were life, liberty, and the pursuit of happiness. Yet the history of mankind was a history of "repeated injuries and usurpations on the part of man toward woman, having in direct object the establishment of a tyranny over her." The Declaration listed some fifteen specific injuries and usurpations—"He has compelled her to submit to laws, in the formation of which she had no voice. . . . He has made her, if married, in the eye of the law, civilly dead"—and insisted that women have "immediate admission to all the rights and privileges which belong to them as citizens of the United States." The women's-righters, then, declared that they acted in behalf of natural rights, the principles of American democracy, and the will of God. Eleven years later John Brown, the notorious abolitionist, said much the same thing shortly before his execution. Convicted by a Virginia court of "treason to the Commonwealth, conspiring with slaves to commit treason and murder," for his work at Harpers Ferry, Brown contended in his speech to the court that he was only doing the work of the Lord. The Bible taught him, Brown said, that "all things whatsoever I would that men should do to me, I should do even so to them. It teaches me, further, to 'remember them that are in bonds, as bound with them.' I endeavored to act up to that instruction." It was the "furtherance of the ends of justice" for which he had acted, so he claimed, and for those ends he was prepared to die.

Although the emphases of the reformers varied—agnostic socialists, for example, did not profess to be obeying the Creator's will—they all claimed to be serving some ultimate good, some higher law, some eternal virtue. The problem facing the student of antebellum reform, however, was to what extent he could believe them. If the reformers' propaganda was sincere, could historians accept it as a true explanation of why they acted? If the propaganda was insincere, what were the reformers' true motives?

Illustrations from one of the more important reform movements, anti-Catholicism, showed the problems that historians faced. During the years from 1830 to 1860 the nation witnessed the rise —and also, happily, the fall—of a great anti-Catholic crusade. It took various forms. Some anti-Catholics were content to issue moderate propaganda arguing that the Bible proved Protestantism right and Romanism wrong. Others lashed out bitterly. They described the Church as the "whore of Babylon" and the "abomination of abominations," they attacked priests and nuns for imaginary sexual perversions, they portrayed the pope as the Antichrist himself or at least as the devil's apostle. Occasionally anti-Catholics turned violent, as did a mob which burned an Ursuline convent in Charlestown, Massachusetts, in 1834. From the 1830s to the 1850s, moreover, both local and national political organizations tried to restrict the power of Catholics and other immigrants as well; their efforts culminated in the American, or Know-Nothing, party which acquired an amazing strength by 1855.

If the historian had to decide merely what the anti-Catholics did and what their justifications for action were, his task would be simple. There have been dozens of monographs; the best is Ray Allen Billington's *The Protestant Crusade, 1800-1860: A Study of the Origins of American Nativism* (New York, 1938). But many historians believed that they had to put anti-Catholicism into the broader reform context. At that point the trouble began. For while anti-Catholics condemned Catholicism, often in the most hateful ways, they professed to be acting in behalf of true Christianity and of American freedom and democracy. Catholicism was allegedly ungodly; fighting it was God's work. Catholicism was allegedly tyrannical; fighting it was part of the battle to preserve liberty. In September, 1833, for example, an editorial in the *Protes-*

tant Magazine, published in New York City, said that Catholicism was a "soul-corrupting, soul-destroying influence," that it was an "anti-Christian" menace to the nation. To "promote the interests of immortal souls" and to save the country from Catholicism's political power, the *Protestant Magazine* intended to defend the "great truths of the gospel opposed by popery, and to exhibit those doctrines and practices of Roman Catholics which are contrary to the interests of mankind."

Few historians were convinced of the anti-Catholics' good faith. Arthur M. Schlesinger, Sr., indeed, did not believe that anti-Catholicism was a reform movement at all. Instead, Schlesinger said, the enemies of Catholicism actually opposed reform. They were the "bigoted enemies" of the principles of the Declaration of Independence and the social teachings of Christianity upon which reform was nourished. Their prejudices and their work were contrary to all that was decent and good in American life. At the opposite pole, however, stood John R. Bodo, author of *The Protestant Clergy and Public Issues, 1812-1848* (Princeton, 1954). Bodo thought anti-Catholicism not only a reform movement, but a desirable reform movement. Although he condemned the liars and the rioters, Bodo said that "The indictment of the Roman Catholic church as being hostile to religious and civil liberty was . . . well-founded." Most historians stood somewhere between Schlesinger and Bodo. They did not approve of anti-Catholicism, they were not certain that the principles of Christianity and natural rights were actually at work in it, but they thought that anti-Catholicism was reform. Ray Allen Billington, though he disliked anti-Catholicism, described it as reform in 1938. Alice Felt Tyler believed it a reform movement that denied the liberties that most other reform movements expressed. It was, she said, among the "almost hysterical denials of the very foundations of American institutions"; it manifested "blind prejudice and mass hatred . . . in refutation of liberal tenets repeatedly affirmed by statesmen and entrenched in the Constitution itself." "Progress toward understanding the full meaning of the democratic faith," Mrs. Tyler wrote murkily, "was not always along the lines of positive assertion." Several other historians—Charles C. Cole, for example, in *The Social Ideas of the Northern Evangelists, 1826-1860* (New York, 1954) and Whitney R. Cross in *The Burned-Over District: The Social and Intellectual History of Enthusiastic Religion in Western New York, 1800-1850* (Ithaca, 1950)—have simply described anti-Catholicism as a reform movement without comparing it with others.

What the student of history had, then, was the problem of whether anti-Catholicism agreed with or contradicted the principles which, for most historians, underlay all antebellum reform. Were anti-Catholics really manifesting Christian and democratic ideals, as other reformers seemed to be, or were they only mouthing those ideals? A disturbing possibility was that if anti-Catholicism was a reform movement, it might be necessary to define reform in a different way from that accepted by the majority of historians. If a denial of what appeared to be Christian and democratic principles was a reform movement, where did that leave a definition of reform that claimed that *in fact* reform was Christianity and democracy in action?

Despite the generally accepted definition of reform, there has been no agreement among historians about the forces and motives which produced the reformers. Some sympathetic men have contended that the reformers simply felt more keenly than their fellow Americans the meaning of Christianity, democracy, the idea of progress, and righteousness in general. The reformer was something of a psychological accident, a person who was, for reasons lying deep within his mind and emotions, especially sensitive to the obvious discrepancies between what was and what ought to be. Writing of Theodore Parker, a zealous abolitionist and transcendentalist, Henry Steele Commager said that by nature Parker possessed "sweetness, gentleness and love for his fellow men, a nobility of mind and a greatness of spirit." Writing of Wendell Phillips, a Massachusetts abolitionist unsurpassed in his hatred of slavery and in his resources of invective, Oscar Sherwin, in his *Prophet of Liberty: The Life and Times of Wendell Phillips* (New York, 1958), said that his hero was a "priceless example of inflexible devotion to conscience and to public duty." "The golden trumpets blow," Sherwin concluded his biography, "and Wendell Phillips rises and stands before the Judgment Seat as Defender of the Poor and Oppressed, Seeker of the Common Good, Knight Errant of Unfriended Truth, and Prophet of Liberty."

Most historians agreed that the reformer was in great part the product of his peculiar psychological condition. But not all of them agreed that it was merely his sensitivity to right and wrong that made him a reformer. In 1942 and again in 1957 Avery Craven questioned that idea in his *The Coming of the Civil War* (New York, 1942; 2d ed., Chicago, 1957). The "modern psychologist," Craven said, was skeptical of ascribing the reformers' zeal only to a "peculiar sensitiveness to wrongdoing—a willingness to sacrifice personal comfort for a larger good." Instead the modern psychologist talked of "youthful experiences, maladjustments, inferiority complexes, and repressed desires." The "student of social affairs" was also "less inclined to grant unstinted praise to the fanatic and is not certain about the value of the contribution. . . . He sees the triumph of emotion over reason in the extremist's course and sometimes wonders if the developments of history might not have been more sound without him. He talks with less assurance about 'progress' in human affairs." In a fascinating study, *On Freedom's Altar: The Martyr Complex in the Abolition Movement* (Madison, 1952), Hazel C. Wolf argued with much evidence that the zeal of many leading antislaveryites came from their eagerness to suffer for their cause. Most Americans abhorred abolitionism, Miss Wolf pointed out, and many Americans attacked the abolitionists both verbally and physically. Outspoken antislaveryites needed great amounts of moral stamina to persevere. But perhaps persecution had its delights and masochism its charms.

The abolitionists were convinced, Miss Wolf wrote, that "if they met opposition with courage they demonstrated their sincerity, that if they bore their sufferings in patience they proved they enjoyed God's favor." She claimed that William Lloyd Garrison was seeking martyrdom, that the vocation of agitator seemed to be the best means to satisfy his enormous desire for persecution and glory. A decade later a biographer of the Massachusetts incendiary repeated Miss Wolf's idea. Walter M. Merrill's *Against Wind and Tide: A Biography of Wm. Lloyd Garrison* (Cambridge, 1963) charged that Garrison's preoccupations were "himself, his persecution, and his probable martyrdom." The idea of martyrdom, indeed, was "central to Garrison's personality."

A different approach to Garrison—and, through him, possibly to many another reformer—appeared in John L. Thomas's *The Liberator: William Lloyd Garrison, A Biography* (Boston, 1963). Garrison was a man who "hungered for recognition," Thomas said, and abolitionism promised him that. More important, however, was Thomas's assertion that the "radical temperament" of both Garrison and other reformers was composed of two not necessarily complementary parts. One part was their nonconformity, their idealism, their concern for the right, whatever the opposition, whatever the opinions of society, whatever the personal cost. But the other part was a powerful authoritarianism, a will to power. Garrison's "view of the world as a vast arena for the struggle between God and the devil," Thomas wrote, "his tenacious anti-intellectualism, and above all, his vision of a perfect and self-regulating society of saints disclosed the longings of an authoritarian mind concerned with getting and using power over others." In a recent reinterpretation of *American Feminists* (Lawrence, 1963) Robert E. Riegel argued that much of the women's rights movement came from a "desire to attain importance and power" by women whose importance and power were slight. "The supporters of women's rights were able and aggressive," Riegel said, "with the usual human desire for recognition. . . . Always there seemed an underlying drive to excel, to show that both the individual and her sex were superior rather than inferior, to justify herself at least to herself, and to produce public evidences of superiority. . . . The feminist movement constituted an important outlet for the urge toward recognition and power that in another period would have found some other expression."

If some reformers sought the delights of persecution and power, both they and others sought the delights of virtue as well—of being on the right side, of experiencing an intimate relation with goodness and with God, of sharing in the happiness that others received once they yielded old lives for new or cast off some oppressive burden. Helen E. Marshall's biography of *Dorothea Dix, Forgotten Samaritan* (Chapel Hill, 1937) demonstrated that Miss Dix was happiest when she was trying to change the wretched lot of the insane and other social outcasts. Miss Dix believed, so she said, that she was "the Hope of the poor crazed things," that she was "the Revelation of hundreds of wailing, suffering creatures," and she gained enormous satisfaction from her work. David Brion Davis has pointed out in "The Emergence of Immediatism in British and American Antislavery Thought" (*Mississippi Valley Historical Review,* XLIX [September, 1962], pp. 209-30) that through the idea of immediate abolitionism many a man found "his own freedom from guilt" and a release from religious anxiety which the traditional churches could not give. "Acceptance of immediatism was the sign of an immediate transformation within the reformer himself; as such, it was seen as an expression of inner freedom, of moral sincerity and earnestness, and of victory over selfish and calculating expediency." "Let the law of the land forge its bonds of wrong," ran an antislavery hymn directed against fugitive slave laws,

> I shall help when the self-freed crave;
> For the law in my soul, bright, beaming, and strong,
> Bids me succor the fleeing slave.

The bright law of virtue beamed in the soul of every reformer and gladdened him as it shone. But if several historians were correct, there were still other motives at work among the reformers. Some of them, at least, hoped that their work would preserve social order, would permit the reformers to continue in positions of moral or social supremacy or to regain a position now lost. In their eyes, change and expansion and tumult seemed to characterize the American nation. The two decades before 1830 had seen the arrival of almost universal white manhood suffrage which in itself was enough to alarm men who favored the control of society by moral or social or economic elites. Many of the newly enfranchised, moreover, favored the popular democracy of Andrew Jackson, which anti-Jacksonians hated because it threatened their own power. The three decades after 1830 saw hundreds of thousands of immigrants inundate American ports as hard times in Ireland, political persecution in Germany, and the promise of America sent them across the Atlantic. Many of the immigrants were poor, many of them were Roman Catholics, most of them were unfamiliar with American institutions—and here was another threat to social stability. More than that, millions of Americans both old and new were pressing westward to conquer the land and find the happiness that had thus far eluded them. As they converted forests and prairies into cities and states, many easterners feared that men in the still-forming western society would be prey to disorder and licentiousness and to the abuse of their ever-growing political power. Even as the West expanded, so did the East, especially the urban centers. From 1840 to 1860 New York City increased its population from 312,000 to 805,000; Philadelphia from 220,000 to 565,000; Boston from 93,000 to 177,000.

For men who feared the lower classes, who feared Jacksonian Democracy, who worried about the West and the immigrants and everything else that they did not control, reform was a means to social order. It was a way of preserving and extending ideas and institutions that had proved their worth in previous years, of guarding against the new by perpetuating the old. A great number of the North's leading clergymen, as Charles C. Cole demonstrated in *The Social Ideas of the Northern Evangelists,* tried to reform men in the name of a conventional Protestant morality. At the same time, however, they strove to convince their congregations and revival audiences that political and economic innovations were contrary to the spirit of the gospel. Such men as Charles Grandison Finney, Lyman Beecher, Henry Ward Beecher, Albert Barnes, and many others fought intemperance, vice, Catholicism, Sabbath profanation, and everything else that seemed to contravene the will of God. But they had no use for Jacksonian Democracy, for labor unions, for universal suffrage, for poor relief on a large scale, or for anything else that seemed to threaten the status quo. They were afraid of the nation's growth, afraid of its change, afraid of that very freedom which other men, as yet unreformed, valued so much. "It was not the moralist's intention for man to be free," Cole wrote, ". . . for he had to be pious, protestant, and pure." These reformers wished to reshape the morality of the masses so that their own middle-class morality might prevail. "Not concerned with the reasons for the existence of poverty, crime, and immorality," Cole said, "the nineteenth-century religious reformers set about to force all men—and women—to live as they."

Other recent students of the relation between religion and antebellum reform have reached essentially the same conclusions, although by different routes. In the same year that Cole's work appeared, John R. Bodo published his study of *The Protestant Clergy and Public Issues, 1812-1848.* Surveying the ideas of a number of eminent clergymen representing the traditional denominations, Bodo found that most of them actually opposed what he called "social reforms"—that is, reforms that would change social institutions to provide better lives for individuals. Thus they fought abolitionism, public education, labor unions, communitarian socialism, and women's rights. Frightened of the consequences of "reforming ideologies," Bodo said, they "consistently advocated the maintenance of the *status quo* in terms of a social and economic paternalism enhanced with the sanctions of religion." Calling his ministers the "theocrats," Bodo argued that they desired to organize the entire nation on their interpretation of Christian principles and to see every individual regenerated according to a conservative interpretation of Holy Writ. At first glance, this might seem to make the theocrats reformers. But Bodo made a distinction between moral reform and social reform, and said that the "only reforms which the theocrats supported were moral reforms, which might have social implications but were directed primarily at the individual. . . . Yet the exercise of such moral criticism cannot properly be called reform, since it involved little or no organized effort and was of slight social consequence."

Although both Cole and Bodo knew that the clerical moral reformers and their lay allies started moral reform societies to make people behave, their emphasis was on individuals. In 1960 two books appeared which redressed the balance by studying a number of organizations whose general goal was to Christianize society. Beginning in 1810, several national voluntary societies had come into existence; their purpose was to make an interdenominational attack on evil. The American Board of Commissioners for Foreign Missions was organized in 1810, the American Bible Society in 1816, the American Sunday School Union in 1824, the American Home Missionary Society—a joint Congregational-Presbyterian effort to supply the nation with neo-Calvinist ministers—in 1826, the American Society for the Promotion of Temperance in 1826; and there were many more. Charles I. Foster's *An Errand of Mercy: The Evangelical United Front, 1790-1837* (Chapel Hill, 1960) and C. S. Griffin's *Their Brothers' Keepers: Moral Stewardship in the United States, 1800-1865* (New Brunswick, 1960) contended that the societies' chief purpose was to make men conform to particular interpretations of morality and decency in order to guard against threatening evil in a changing age. The object of the societies, Foster said, was the "conversion of every American and, beyond that, of every non-Evangelical person in the entire world." Conversion would provide a "conservative counterbalance to native radicalism" and produce conformity to the precepts of the societies' leaders. Griffin made the same point. The leaders, he wrote, believed that the "spread of the Protestant gospel and the pervasive influence of Protestant morality would not only save the souls of their fellow citizens, but would restore to men and to society, stability and order, sobriety and safety."

Running parallel to the ideas of Cole, Bodo, Foster, and Griffin was a secularized version of their thesis offered by David Donald in 1956. In a chapter of his *Lincoln Reconsidered: Essays on the Civil War Era* (New York) called "Toward a Reconsideration of Abolitionists," Donald argued that many abolitionists had become reformers because the social class to which they belonged was losing both prestige and power. Abolitionism—and other kinds of reform as well—was a means of getting them back. Claiming to have investigated 106 abolitionists, "the hard core of active antislavery leadership in the 1830s," Donald said that most of them were of New England extraction. More important, he said that their parents "generally belonged to a clearly defined stratum of society." They were preachers, doctors, teachers, farmers, merchants; they represented old and distinguished New England families; almost all of them were staunch Federalists. They had been leaders in their communities, Donald wrote, and their descendants expected to be the same. But in the 1830s those descendants faced a "strange and hostile world" in which social and economic leadership was passing "from the country to the city, from the farmer to the manufacturer, from the preacher to the corporation attorney. . . . Expecting to lead, these young people found no followers. They were an elite without function, a displaced class in American society." Through reform, then, they sought a "reassertion of their traditional values," association with others of their kind, "that self-fulfillment which should traditionally have been theirs as social leaders. . . . Basically, abolitionism should be considered the anguished protest of an aggrieved class against a world they never made."

Donald's essay, alas, was long on speculation and short on evidence. He did not name his abolitionists, and thus no one could tell who their parents had been, or to what social class they had belonged. He could not—or would not—prove that their social displacement had led them to reform. All in all, as Robert A. Skotheim pointed out in a critical article entitled "A Note on Historical Method: David Donald's 'Toward a Reconsideration of Abolitionists'" (*Journal of Southern History,* XXV [August, 1959], pp. 356-65), the thesis as it stood was unacceptable. Here and there, however, an historian did accept it, either in whole or in part. Lawrence Lader's *The Bold Brahmins: New England's War against Slavery, 1831-1863* (New York, 1961) and Oscar Sherwin's *Prophet of Liberty* repeated it. Stanley M. Elkins's *Slavery: A Problem in American Institutional and Intellectual Life* (Chicago, 1959) praised it. Merton L. Dillon's *Elijah P. Lovejoy* admitted its validity but quickly pointed out that there was more to reform than an effort to regain a "declining status: there was evil in the world," Dillon said, and religious New Englanders "felt a responsibility to do something about it." Most historians, however, either rejected the Donald thesis or remained skeptical as they awaited proof.

THE SECTIONAL PROBLEM

When Donald contended that his "hard core" of antislavery leaders were mostly New Englanders or descendants of New England families, he rubbed a spot on the body historical already sore from years of irritation. Historians have long been arguing about whether reform was a New England product or a product of other parts of the North. The New England syndrome appeared in different forms. Some historians urged that New England transcendentalism was largely responsible for the reform impulse. To an "astonishing degree," said Henry Steele Commager in *The Era of Reform,* the reform movement was the "product of . . . Transcendentalism." In *The Idea of Progress in America, 1815-1860* (New York, 1944), still the best study of the concept, Arthur A. Ekirch alleged that in the 1840s transcendentalism became the "popular reform philosophy of the day." By placing its "emphasis on moral and individual progress," Ekirch said, transcendentalism "gave hope to those who were distressed by the materialism of the rising industrial order." Arthur Y. Lloyd, in *The Slavery Controversy, 1831-1860* (Chapel Hill, 1939), claimed that "humanitarianism, idealism, and transcendentalism dominated the philosophy of the time." In *Fettered Freedom* Russel B. Nye used Lloyd's words, but added "liberalism" to the list. Historians inclined to view New England more broadly have written of the famous New England conscience, of the New Englanders' concern for both morality and freedom, as the impetus to antebellum reform. Thus Otelia Cromwell's biography of the feminist leader *Lucretia Mott* (Cambridge, 1958) said that the six-state region was the center of American reform because of the New Englanders' concern for righteousness and their "ideals of liberty and education." The New England emphasis was especially strong among the historians who believed that the abolition movement owed most of its vigor to William Lloyd Garrison and his followers. Ralph Korngold's emotion-laden account of *Two Friends of Man: The Story of William Lloyd Garrison and Wendell Phillips and Their Relationship with Abraham Lincoln* (Boston, 1950) made Garrison the "sower who went forth to sow and whose seed fell onto fertile ground, blossoming forth in a variety of shapes." Garrison was the "spiritual father of innumerable children," Korngold said, "most of whom disowned him. He shamed a reluctant nation into doing what it did not wish to do." In 1961 Lawrence Lader's *The Bold Brahmins* asserted that Garrison "whipped and goaded the conscience of a people," that his voice "shattered the 'conspiracy of silence' that had lasted from 1820 to 1831."

No one could deny, of course, that New Englanders played important roles in all sorts of reform movements. There was Garrison himself, the best known abolitionist of his day. There was Neal Dow, the instigator of the Maine prohibition law of 1851. There was Horace Mann, the nation's greatest champion of common schools. In Vermont there was John Humphrey Noyes, who would perfect both man and society; in Massachusetts there were George Ripley and his Brook Farmers; in Connecticut there was Prudence Crandall, who in 1833 admitted a Negro to her private school in Canterbury and then, when white parents withdrew their children, turned the school into one for Negroes only.

But the work of the New England reformers did not mean that all antebellum reform had its origins in New England nor did the presence of transcendentalism there explain the reform spirit. The transcendentalists themselves made no such claims. Looking back on transcendentalism half a century later, Ralph Waldo Emerson remembered that it was no movement, no concert of the like-minded propagandizing a cause. Those whom the world called transcendentalists—no one knew, Emerson said, who originated the name or when it was first applied—were merely men and women who had a few similar ideas, who had read Coleridge, Wordsworth, Goethe, and Carlyle, and who discussed and wrote about their ideas from time to time. The so-called "transcendentalists," Emerson stated, had different ideas on almost every conceivable subject. In 1852 William Henry Channing, a disciple of the transcendentalist Margaret Fuller, said much the same thing. Only the "mere attraction of affinity" drew the transcendentalists together; what they had in common was only a "hopeful and liberal spirit." Perceptive historians have made the same point. "Erratic, sophisticated, and at odds with popular religious prejudices," said Timothy L. Smith, transcendentalism's champions "were as much inclined to withdraw from the world as they were to reform it." Carl Bode in *The Anatomy of American Popular Culture, 1840-1861* (Berkeley, 1959) said that no historian would "assert that Transcendentalism had a marked influence on mass attitudes. . . . Aside from Emerson, disciples of the new movement aroused more hostility than friendship in the crowd." Despite the constant use that Arthur M. Schlesinger, Sr., made of Ralph Waldo Emerson's ideas in *The American as Reformer,* he did not mention transcendentalism as a cause of reform.

Many other historians have denied that New England was the only home, or even the most important dwelling, of the reform impulse. In 1933 Gilbert H. Barnes tried to cure the New England syndrome in his *The Antislavery Impulse, 1830-1844* (New York). Writing with as much passion as judgment, and including other reforms along with antislaveryism, Barnes claimed that western New York and the middle states generally had been a far more fruitful seedbed of reform than New England. It was from the middle states, he said, that the reforming spirit had spread to the Middle West. The dominant force behind reform in the 1830s, Barnes claimed, was a tremendous evangelical religious revival generated by one of the greatest preachers of his day, the Reverend Charles Grandison Finney. Possessing in full measure everything the compleat revivalist needed—superabundant energy, a striking figure, a splendid invective for condemning sin, a hyperactive imagination in portraying the horrors of hell and the delights of heavenly virtue, a magnificent compassion, and perhaps even divine inspiration (who could tell?)—Finney ranged across New York and surrounding areas preaching the gospel of benevolence and reform. His converts he charged with the divine duty of divine love: to be benevolent to other men by turning them from the primrose path into the ways of the Lord. Around him Finney gathered a "holy band" of moral reformers who strove to prove the reality of their conversion to Christ by redeeming others. To Finney's western "new-born converts and their rejoicing brethren fresh from the ardor of revival," Barnes said, "social ills seemed easily curable and dreams of reform were future realities." Undeniably, Barnes had a point. If New Englanders were important reformers, so were New Yorkers, and so were Ohioans and other men in the transappalachian West, where the spirit of the revival moved in full measure. But Barnes went on to overstress his point. The heart of the reform spirit in New England and the West alike, he said, was in the churches. William Lloyd Garrison and men like him were contemptuous of most churches—and of most Christians, too—for opposing or refusing to cooperate with the abolitionists. So the true reform impulse was "not in the noisy futilities of the Boston reformers, but in the expanding benevolence of the Great Revival."

Barnes made a number of converts of his own. In the first volume of his immense *Ordeal of the Union* (2 vols., New York, 1947), Allan Nevins argued that his predecessors had overemphasized William Lloyd Garrison's importance. Accepting the Barnes thesis, Nevins claimed that "by far the greater public influence" for antislaveryism "was exercised by the New Yorkers and Westerners." In 1950 Benjamin P. Thomas published a valuable biography of *Theodore Weld: Crusader for Freedom* (New Brunswick). Weld was one of Finney's converts and in the 1830s the foremost propagandist of the American Anti-Slavery Society. Admitting that Garrison had been important, Thomas yet denied that he was "typical of the antislavery agitator." The New Yorkers and the westerners had given antislaveryism "its most effective impulse." When Dwight L. Dumond, a friend and associate of Gilbert H. Barnes, published his *Antislavery* in 1961, he largely neglected Garrison and emphasized the New Yorkers and westerners instead.

It was inevitable that some historian should try to work out an accommodation—if not a synthesis—between eastern and western champions. In 1963 John L. Thomas contended in *The Liberator,* the best biography of Garrison, that both the New Englanders and Finney's benevolent offspring were important to abolitionism and moral reform in general. But the western leaders, Thomas said, were actually "transplanted New Englanders, like Theodore Weld, Beriah Green, Elizur Wright, and Henry Stanton," who drank deep at the Garrisonian springs. In 1833, Thomas said, the transplanted and the stay-at-home New Englanders joined to form the American Anti-Slavery Society under the leadership of a wealthy New York City reformer named Arthur Tappan, himself a native of Massachusetts. Thomas made much of the general fervor of reform in New England; although he presented no extravagant claims for the region as the only source of the reform spirit, it was the main source of abolitionism.

The wisdom of hindsight suggests, however, that the regional sources of reform were less important than the personal sources. If the New England environment produced hundreds of zealous reformers, it also produced their zealous opponents. Except for the abolitionists and the nativists, moreover, the New England reformers were fighting evils indigenous to the region itself. It was New Englanders, after all, who in 1835 dragged William Lloyd Garrison through the streets of Boston and threatened to kill him. It was tippling New Englanders who inspired much of the temperance crusade; it was slothful New Englanders whom Horace Mann tried to awaken to the need for school reform; it was New England males perpetuating their male dominance whom the feminists fought. The same was true for other regions of the nation in which reformers were active. Obviously the social and intellectual environment was an important influence on reform. Just as obviously the effect of any environment upon an individual depended in great part on the way in which the individual received it, upon his predispositions, his character, his perceptions. The nature of a particular environment for any reformer, indeed, was less an objective reality than it was the idea of the reformer himself.

The problem of environment has troubled historians in still another way. On the whole they have seen antebellum reform as a northern phenomenon and have neglected its southern expressions. By the mid-1960s there was no comprehensive study of antebellum reform in the slave states, nor was there a book that attempted to present an integrated account of northern and southern reform. Occasionally an historian has claimed that there was no southern reform movement at all. "Everywhere (except in the South)," wrote Eleanor Flexner in her *Century of Struggle: The Woman's Rights Movement in the United States* (Cambridge, 1959), "horizons were broadening, old ways being re-tested, new ideas fermenting." John Hope Franklin's *From Slavery to Freedom: A History of American Negroes* (2d ed., New York, 1956) claimed that the plantation system tended to preserve "frontier independence" in the antebellum South. Hence, Franklin said, "there was no communal life, no civic responsibility, and no interest in various programs for the improvement of mankind." A number of studies both older and more recent made it plain that there had once been an important antislavery movement south of Mason and Dixon's line. But southern antislaveryism had declined with the rise of the northern movement, as everyone knew. Most historians seemed to believe that if there was no very strong abolition movement in the South, there was no strong reform movement in general. The South as a field for investigation was largely neglected.

Yet there were many southern reformers, as a minority of historians have recognized. In the 1820s and the 1830s, and in later decades as well, Charles S. Sydnor pointed out in *The Development of Southern Sectionalism, 1819-1848* (Baton Rouge, 1948), southerners championed more schools and colleges, improvement of public health, the creation of libraries, the reformation of criminal codes, the improvement of prisons, and more humane treatment for debtors. Helen E. Marshall's biography of Dorothea Dix demonstrated that Miss Dix found widespread southern support for her crusade to improve the lot of the insane. Harold Schwartz's fine study of *Samuel Gridley Howe: Social Reformer, 1801-1876* (Cambridge, 1956) showed that southerners were receptive to Howe's pleas for money and help for the blind. Others have pointed out that southerners eagerly backed the temperance

movement, as they did Bible and tract distribution and moral reform generally. Although reform did move at a slower pace in the
South than in the North and although the North certainly had
more varieties of reform than the South, it was certain that reform
was never sectional. Yet it still remains for an historian to explore
all the dimensions of southern reform and to integrate it with
antebellum reform elsewhere.

EVERYMAN A REFORMER— AND A CONSERVATIVE?

More important, however, it also remains for some historian to
write an integrated account of the reform spirit generally. In 1951
Arthur M. Schlesinger, Sr., in *The American as Reformer,* had
offered his thoughts about reform in American history not as a
final statement on the matter, but in hope of stimulating further
research. "The American as reformer is inescapably present in
every extensive account of American history," Schlesinger said,
"for such has been the nature of the people who settled and built
the Republic. Few historians if any, however, have specifically examined the general character and workings of the reform impulse."
During the fifteen years after Schlesinger wrote, his words continued to be true both for American history in general and for
antebellum history in particular—except for Alice Felt Tyler's
Freedom's Ferment. Since Mrs. Tyler's general account of 1944,
many monographs had appeared which put her book—interesting
and valuable though it remained—in need of revision. By the mid-
1960s, moreover, there had also appeared ideas, admittedly only
partially formed, that suggested that historians had been much too
restrictive in their definitions of reform and reformers. Possibly the
time had come to reopen the questions of what reform was, and
who reformers were.

Whatever the differences of opinion that existed about the
idea of reform, the historians generally agreed that reform was a

peculiar kind of activity, and the reformer a unique kind of person. Implicitly rather than explicitly historians divided antebellum Americans into three groups: the reformers, their opponents, and people who cared nothing one way or another about reform. In most of the literature, temperance men and prohibitionists were reformers, but the liquor drinkers who fought them and tried to repeal their laws were not. Labor union organizers were reformers, but the owners and managers who fought them were not. A reformer was, for most historians, a person who tried to implement the teachings of Christianity and the theory of the Declaration of Independence. Therefore the abolitionist who desired to eliminate slavery in the name of those ideals was a reformer; but the slaveholder, who justified slavery by the Bible and by natural law, and who was eager to reform the abolitionists by countering their ideas and decreasing their influence, was a nonreformer. On the whole the millions of ordinary Americans, nameless to history, who subdued nature and pursued happiness and built a nation all in the name of Christianity and natural law and democracy, were not really reformers either, except as they joined one of the various "crusades" or "causes" of the day.

The question that a few contemporary historians are asking is whether *all* men might be reformers, at least insofar as they strive to alter any existing condition in order to make things better. "Reform may be defined broadly as the effort by words and deeds to change and improve upon existing conditions," wrote Charles L. Sanford in "Classics of American Reform Literature" (*American Quarterly,* X [Fall, 1958], pp. 295-311). "In this sense, American reforming zeal is not confined to spasmodic social protest movements or eccentric experiments but is characteristic of the American people generally, whatever their class or sectional interests. For some three centuries they have been enlisted in a 'permanent revolution' dedicated to progress, to social and individual betterment, variously interpreted." In 1963 Louis Filler made some interesting observations about the problem in his *A Dictionary of*

American Social Reform (New York). Reform, he said, was a "concept which has inspired or depressed individuals and generations, suggesting hope and fresh approaches to some, half-measures to others; it has differed from revolution in its concern for existing conditions, rather than new principles." If this was not overly enlightening, some of Filler's other statements about reform were most suggestive. "Anti-reform has often been a species of reform, concerned for the state of society, urgent in its demand for a return to allegedly better conditions." So-called "conservatism" could be reform, for "Conservatives have often sought change, in order to preserve the principles they defended." And Filler called brief attention in his preface to *The Reformer,* an antebellum publication fighting the reforms of its day. "*The Reformer* . . . was opposed to reform: that was its reform."

Ralph Waldo Emerson was more provocative still. In his lecture "The Conservative," delivered in Boston in December, 1841, Emerson argued that every man was a reformer at some time in his life—and that every man was a conservative at other times. The two parties which then divided men, "the party of Conservatism and that of Innovation" or reform, were reflections of a dualism that existed in the human constitution itself. Each person was a combination of a desire for the new and a predilection for the old; within each existed the "opposition of Past and Future, of Memory and Hope," of an acceptance of what was and an idealism that made man yearn for what ought to be. There was no such thing as a "pure conservative," for every person when conditions were right "espouses for the time the cause of man; and even if this be a shortlived emotion, yet the remembrance of it in private hours mitigates his selfishness and compliance with custom." There was no such thing as a "pure reformer," either, for what else was a reformer doing than attempting to make his own ideas prevail forever, and was not this the essence of conservatism? "You quarrel with my conservatism," Emerson said to the reformers, "but it is to build up one of your own; . . . among the lovers of the new

I observe that there is a jealousy of the newest, and that the seceder from the seceder is as damnable as the pope himself." It was also true, Emerson said, that every reformer used the traditions and ideas of the past to gain his vision of the future. The hope of a better world was "not imported from the stock of some celestial plant, but grew here on the wild crab of conservatism." Man could not live by reform or by conservatism alone. In a "true society, in a true man, both must combine."

If Emerson was right, antebellum reform and, indeed, the antebellum Americans needed a much different kind of analysis than historians have given them. For if every man at some time is a reformer, the history of reform becomes the history of an aspect of human nature, rather than the study of particular groups, movements, and men who are thought to be different from their fellow citizens. And if every reformer—that is to say, every man—is also a conservative, and if reform activities are often the expression of conservatism, then reform itself needs considerable redefinition.

Well over a century after Emerson wrote, however, historians have not accepted his ideas, even as hypotheses for further investigation. They remain merely the intriguing notions of one thoughtful observer of antebellum reform. But the modern historians have agreed with Emerson that antebellum reform had a remarkable variety of expressions. In writing of that variety, they have contributed much to a better understanding of the American character in the years before the Civil War.

TWO

Some Varieties of Reform Experience

NEW DIRECTIONS AFTER 1830

Whatever reform was, it was nothing new in 1830. The party of Conservatism and the party of Innovation, Emerson said correctly, were "very old, and have disputed the possession of the world ever since it was made. . . . The war rages not only in battle-fields, in national councils and ecclesiastical synods, but agitates every man's bosom with opposing advantages every hour. On rolls the old world meantime, and now one, now the other gets the day, and still the fight renews itself as if for the first time, under new names and hot personalities."

Looking backward from 1830, it was clear that much of American history had been made by reformers, by men seeking to change ideas and institutions in the name of a higher ethic and secular happiness. The principles of moral and religious reform had sent Pilgrims and Puritans westering to the New World, there to build the Kingdom of God; had sent Thomas Hooker and Roger Williams from Massachusetts into the wilderness; had sent William Penn and his fellow Quakers to Pennsylvania. In the name of natural rights and Christian principles Americans resisted English control in the seventeenth and eighteenth centuries and at last declared their independence. Historians would apparently argue forever about the reasons why the Founding Fathers wrote the Constitution of 1787, but it was clear that the Fathers wished to reform conditions they thought undesirable. And it required no deep insight into American history to see that from the start of the colonial period thousands of disadvantaged Americans had fought their actual and would-be persecutors in the name of religious freedom, of material happiness, of political democracy, of everything that constituted virtue and the good life.

Yet by the early 1830s there were newer aspects to reform: newer approaches, emphases, techniques, and even ideas. No historian, of course, would claim that the great antebellum reform impulse began suddenly in 1830 or in the next few years; the impulse had numerous antecedents in the past. By the 1830s, however, reform had assumed characteristics that would distinguish it for the next three decades. One of the more important characteristics was that reform was national—national in vision, national in goals, national in operations. Merely the names of various organizations made the point. It was the *American* Colonization Society, the *American* Peace Society, the *American* Society for the Promotion of Temperance, the *American* Anti-Slavery Society, and a hundred more. Such names reflected the reformers' dual purpose. On the one hand, they desired to cleanse the entire nation of evil, to extend to all the nation's citizens the virtue, happiness, and progress that were inherent in the reformers' ideas. This was true even for the northern abolitionists, whom first glance might see as working to eliminate an institution peculiar to one section of the country. If slavery was a southern institution by the 1830s, abolitionists argued that the guilt for slavery was nationwide. The founders of the American Anti-Slavery Society maintained in 1833 that "in view of the civil and religious privileges of this nation, the guilt of its oppression is unequalled by any other on the face of the earth; and, therefore, that it is bound to repent instantly, to undo the heavy burdens, and to let the oppressed go free." Guilt was national, repentance should be national, and so the abolitionists contended that there were "at the present time, the highest obligations resting upon the people of the free States to remove slavery by moral and political action, as prescribed in the Constitution of the United States." Even the most visionary reformers had a broad national view. "Our freer, but yet far from freed, land," Bronson Alcott wrote in 1842, "is the asylum, if asylum there be, for the hope of man; and there, if anywhere, is the second Eden to be planted in which the divine seed is to bruise the head of Evil and restore Man to his rightful communion with God in the Paradise of Good." To plant at least one seed of the second Eden, Alcott, his family, his English friend Charles Lane, and several others began an experiment in communal living in Massachusetts, which they named Fruitlands. Thanks to Alcott's dreamy impracticality and to the members' growing hatred of Lane's dictatorial ways, the seed shriveled and then disappeared. But for a time Bronson Alcott had hoped that his experiment might begin to alter the entire nation.

The ferment of reform was national, on the other hand, in that most leading reformers sought the fellowship and support of like-minded men and women throughout the land. Conversely,

Americans everywhere who worked for a particular reform became increasingly conscious of their moral and intellectual kinship. Until 1851, for example, Neal Dow worked most effectively for prohibition in his native Maine, though he kept well informed about the cold-water crusade elsewhere and spoke elsewhere for the cause. But after the passage of his so-called "Maine Law" in 1851, as Frank L. Byrne has described so well in *Prophet of Prohibition: Neal Dow and His Crusade* (Madison, 1961), Dow became a symbol to prohibitionists everywhere in America and in England as well. The Maine Law was the nation's first statewide prohibition ordinance. Prohibitionists in other states made Dow a cold-water hero, imported him to describe the law's successes Down East and urge passage of similar laws in their own commonwealths, and through him gave greater strength to a campaign long since national in outlook. National reform societies not only spread their propaganda and sent their agents scurrying across the nation, but organized thousands of local societies as auxiliaries in one way or another to the parent organization, and tried to incorporate unaffiliated local groups into the national network. Not that cooperation between the national and local societies was always harmonious. By the late 1830s auxiliaries of the American Anti-Slavery Society had become much annoyed by the Society's traveling agents whose exhortations to ceaseless activity always ended with an appeal for money to be sent to national headquarters in New York. In the late 1850s relations between the American Tract Society in New York and its large branch in Boston became so strained over the refusal of the New York officers to issue antislavery propaganda that the New Englanders seceded from the national organization and set up publishing on their own.

The nationalization of reform was both a result and a cause of the growing national spirit in the United States as a whole. It was part of an increasing sense of national identity, a sense still imperfect yet ever more pervasive as the years passed. Antebellum reformers alike drew upon and stimulated the national spirit. Their predecessors in the seventeenth and eighteenth centuries had looked most often to a locality, a colony, at best a region; even in the early nineteenth century reform was mainly local in scope. But the reform emphasis changed because it had to change, because the idea of local reform was meaningless in an increasingly nationalistic age. Encouraged by the progress of the past and heartened by the promise of the future, the reformers strove to convince the unredeemed that the nation as a nation was not what it should be, that all Americans should join their efforts to convert dream into reality.

A second important characteristic of reform was that it was organized in multitudes of national and local voluntary societies. Now voluntary organization for human improvement was no new idea. In the eighteenth and early nineteenth centuries Americans had created an amazing number of societies ranging in purpose and scope from the American Philosophical Society in Philadelphia and the American Academy of Arts and Sciences in Boston to various public or semipublic library associations to missionary and moral reform groups. The national associations of a later day were natural extensions of the earlier organizations. But the antebellum voluntary societies, as Arthur M. Schlesinger, Sr., pointed out in "Biography of a Nation of Joiners" (*American Historical Review,* L [October, 1944], pp. 1-25), reflected a changed and changing America. Many of the national groups were larger and more influential than the earlier ones because the cities in which they stood were larger than ever before and because the nation's financial resources had greatly increased. The older societies, moreover, had usually been controlled and supported by social and economic elites. Wealthy and powerful men often directed the new organizations, too, but they solicited members and contributors from all the people; thus they expressed a growing democratic spirit and joined men of common interests and purposes amid a diversity of peoples. There were also organizations begun and operated by men who themselves were suffering, or had suffered in the recent past, from various oppressions. The idea that in America a man could continually improve his lot led naturally to the notion that improvement would be faster if undertaken through democratic cooperation. Thus it was that hundreds of local trade societies or unions appeared; in 1834 representatives of various national craft unions formed the National Trades' Union. In 1840 half a dozen topers in Baltimore, converted from their cups by a temperance lecturer, swore off booze forever and formed the Washington Temperance Society to reform their former fellow drunkards everywhere.

In their very existence and in their work, the societies expressed their members' disenchantment with traditional institutions as the only means of individual and social reform. Although many reformers would continue to work through the churches, would continue to use the agencies of government and political parties to help in the nation's reformation, they believed those institutions alone inadequate for final victory. The need for reform was so imperative, the reformers so eager to win the day, that they could not abide the slow pace at which the existing institutions worked. The reformers' causes, moreover, were causes that often seemed to transcend the narrower interests of religious denominations and partisan politics. There were temperance and peace and antislavery men in every church and every party, for example, but it was the societies rather than the churches or parties that offered the best means for uniting their work. What many reformers sought were organizations with a single purpose to replace, or to supplement, older institutions whose nature and purposes were diffuse, whose activities could not be properly focused. Some reformers— most obviously the abolitionists—would use their organizations to gain political leverage. For where evil institutions rested on evil laws, the reformers had to engage in political action. But wherever a voluntary society existed, it meant that its officers and members believed that other institutions were deficient and that something more was needed.

Both the societies and the country's increasing prosperity made possible the appearance of a new social type: the professional reformer, the man who could give reform his full time because there was a living in it for himself and his family. The great majority of reformers, of course, continued to be amateurs—that is, men and women who reformed for the love of it. Most of the leaders of the moral reform societies were business and professional men; most of the members were citizens whose livelihoods did not depend upon reform. Most antislaveryites, most women's-righters, most nativists were nonprofessionals; and most of the clergymen among the reformers received the usual stipends from their congregations. Other reformers, however, were men who did nothing else, whose personal prosperity depended on the vigor of their crusade, the sales receipts from their reform publications, the charity of their sympathizers. No reformer, clearly, became rich through reform. William Lloyd Garrison was often on the edge of extreme poverty; yet he managed to get by, thanks to his friends' frequent help. Faring better than Garrison were many of the paid secretaries of the national moral reform organizations such as the American Bible Society and the American Tract Society. Publishing and selling great quantities of Scriptures, tracts, and books, and zealously soliciting contributions, the societies paid their secretaries about $1,200 a year in the 1830s and over $2,000 annually in the 1850s; the salaries were considerably greater than those of most of the nation's workingmen and even most of the nation's ministers. Had there been no professional reformers, the reform impulse generally would have been the loser; the fact that many men could devote all their efforts to reform gave the impulse much of its vigor.

Still another significant aspect of much of antebellum American reform was that it owed much to foreign examples and foreign reformers—especially the British. What Frank Thistlethwaite has called *The Anglo-American Connection in the Early Nineteenth Century* (Philadelphia, 1959) still remains imperfectly treated and imperfectly understood as it concerned the reform movements; there is no detailed synthesis of the relations between the American reformers and their British counterparts. But Charles I. Foster's *Errand of Mercy* made it plain that a number of British evangelical reformers and reform societies—such as the members of the so-called "Clapham Sect," the London Missionary Society, the British and Foreign Bible Society, and the London Religious Tract Society—gave example and inspiration to the Americans. Robert Owen and Frances Wright, the two most famous utopian socialists of the 1820s, were both Britishers. Two of the nation's foremost temperance advocates in the 1840s were immigrants: John B. Gough was a native of Kent and Father Theobald Mathew, a Catholic priest who toured the nation from 1849 to 1851, was an Irishman. Before and after 1830 British abolitionists encouraged the Americans to intensify their attack on slavery. Men such as George Bourne, Charles Stuart, and George Thompson crossed the Atlantic to spur on their fellow reformers. The founders of the American Anti-Slavery Society had long known of the ideas and work of eminent British antislaveryites such as Thomas Clarkson, Granville Sharp, and William Wilberforce, and of the British Anti-Slavery Society's efforts to abolish human bondage in the English colonies and throughout the world. Passage by Parliament in 1833 of a bill to end slavery in the West Indies strengthened the Americans' determination to begin a national society. Throughout the 1830s, and into the 1840s and 1850s, American abolitionists continued to look to Great Britain for material aid and moral support; and during the Civil War the Britishers' antislavery attitudes would aid the northern cause. While some reformers drew upon Great Britain, a few others drew upon France. In the 1840s the communitarian socialism of Charles Fourier had a considerable vogue. Albert Brisbane and Horace Greeley became his chief American apologists, and from 1845 to 1847 the Brook Farm community in Massachusetts was a Fourierist phalanx. Many Americans were suspicious of all things European, and especially of all things English, but reformers knew that goodness was international rather than national and that virtue was where one found it.

All these factors gave antebellum reform a vigor and a significance that reform had lacked during the colonial and early national periods. Two other characteristics increased its importance the more. One of them was that the reformers of the period between 1830 and 1860 hoped and expected to win their final victories in a very short time. Full of romantic optimism—and full of romantic naïveté as well—they believed no obstacles were insuperable, that the ultimate triumph was close at hand. On the whole the reformers of an earlier day had known that achieving their goals would take time. Although the Massachusetts Puritan leaders, for example, had hoped to create and maintain a godly community from the start, they knew that every man—even God's elect—had the old Adam within him, and that devising a perfect society of perfect men was impossible. A century later Jonathan Edwards, the greatest evangelical religious reformer of his age, rejoiced in the work that God was doing through him and his religious revivals to bring sinners to Christ. Yet sensible man that he was, Edwards knew that infidelity in its various forms was on the rise, and that the enthusiasm of his revival audiences was not necessarily a token of God's spirit at work within them. If the final victory might one day come, its day was not yet in sight. Similarly, the leaders of the American antislavery movement from the 1790s through the 1820s were mostly gradualistic in approach. Slavery might be immediately and absolutely wrong, the slaves entitled to their freedom at once, but the processes of manumission, they thought, should go forward slowly. All sorts of proposals suggested themselves, as Alice D. Adams pointed out in *The Neglected Period of Anti-Slavery in America, 1808-1831* (Boston, 1908). Some men would have philanthropists buy slaves to set them free; others thought that colonizing the freed Negroes in Africa was the answer; still others would begin a campaign of moral education for the whites or try to induce southern legislatures to compensate owners who freed slaves. Whatever the method, abolitionists knew that slavery was a most complex institution and that dealing with those complexities was not the work of a moment.

The temperament of most reformers in the late eighteenth and early nineteenth centuries was what later generations would call "realistic." Like their successors after 1830, of course, the earlier reformers were eager to show their fellow citizens where they erred and to complete their reformation. But their reason told them—whether that reason was an accompaniment of traditional Protestant ideas or whether it was the reason of the Enlightenment—that men and institutions were not rapidly perfectible. Their reason told them that they should work mainly through existing institutions, that they should carefully study the laws of nature and of nature's God before deciding plans of action, that wholesale or immediate social change was alike impossible and undesirable.

Yet amid that rationalistic, gradualistic spirit a new and contrary spirit was being born. Increasing numbers of men and women began to doubt that the millennium was as remote as so many of their predecessors and contemporaries believed. Well over a century later historians still had trouble explaining the rise and spread of the immediatist and perfectionist spirit that so many antebellum reformers had. Part of that spirit was surely owing to the appearance of a post-Revolutionary, post-Constitutional generation that matured in an age that seemed bright with hope. In the 1830s an older generation of reformers was giving way to a younger. Ralph Waldo Emerson was born in 1803; Neal Dow in 1804; William Lloyd Garrison and Joseph Smith, the founder of Mormonism, in 1805; Charles Sumner, Horace Greeley, Wendell Phillips, and John Humphrey Noyes in 1811; Harriet Beecher Stowe in 1812; Henry David Thoreau in 1817. Now there was no point whatever in trying to see reform after 1830 only as the product of youthful enthusiasm. It was true, however, that many antebellum reformers grew to adulthood in an age that most of their predecessors had not known. It took no great perception for a young man or woman to see that the Americans generally were rapidly changing their nation for the better. There was an enormous economic boom in the 1820s and 1830s, and an even greater one in the 1840s and 1850s; the nation's recovery from the Panic of 1837 and the depression that followed seemed to prove that the economy was sound, after all. While the population increased, while settlers pushed the frontier westward, while political democracy became a reality, while men invented new labor-saving machines and developed better means of transportation and communication, it appeared that the rate of progress was constantly accelerating. And from the mouths and pens of thousands of politicians and newspaper editors, clergymen and businessmen, came the same message: that the future was bound to be better than the past, that America was finally free of Europe's corruption and decadence, that only in the United States was man's pursuit of happiness likely to be successful.

Reinforcing economic and political progress, reinforcing the idea of America's moral superiority, were important religious and spiritual changes which the youthful reformers—and the reformers who were always young at heart, like William Ellery Channing—at once drew upon and nourished. In a new age and a new environment many older religious ideas and practices seemed unsatisfactory. Although the Americans collectively manifested virtually all the traditional varieties of Protestantism, in growing numbers they repudiated those varieties that emphasized a separation between man and God. An existing orthodox Calvinism would continue to produce reformers, as would orthodox Unitarianism, Episcopalianism, and the more conservative forms of Methodism; the beliefs of every Protestant denomination held principles that could sustain some kind of reform. What mattered more and more, however, was that men should feel a closeness to the Almighty, should feel the Lord's spirit dwelling within them. Naturally enough the desired proximity to God took different forms with different men. "Standing on the bare ground—my head bathed by the blithe air and uplifted into infinite space," Ralph Waldo Emerson wrote in *Nature* (Boston, 1836), "—all mean egotism vanishes. I become a transparent eyeball; I am nothing; I see all; the currents of the Universal Being circulate through me; I am part or parcel of God." While Emerson and other transcendentalists urged a similar ecstatic communion with God on other men, the Reverend Charles Grandison Finney urged his revival audiences to open their souls so that the Lord might enter in and save them. Throughout his life Finney remembered the joy of his own conversion in 1821; it was his own vision of communion with God that he would have other men share. After determining to accept Christ, he seemed to meet Jesus "face to face" in the back room of his law office in Adams, New York. After weeping for himself and confessing his sins, Finney believed himself baptized anew by the Holy Spirit. "The Holy Spirit descended upon me in a manner that seemed to go through me, body and soul," he wrote later. "I could feel the impression, like a wave of electricity, going through and through me." It seemed to come in "waves and waves of liquid love," it seemed like the "very breath of God," it seemed to fan him "like immense wings." "I wept aloud with joy and love; and I do not know but I should say, I literally bellowed out the unutterable gushings of my heart. These waves came over me, and over me, and over me, one after the other, until I recollect I cried out, 'I shall die if these waves continue to pass over me.' I said, 'Lord, I cannot bear any more'; yet I had no fear of death." Out upon a sinful world he went, and his waves—or were they God's?—rolled over upstate New York and washed far beyond. Finney would later pass into still another kind of intimate communion with God, called perfectionism. As defined by John Humphrey Noyes, its leading exponent, perfectionism meant that men could free themselves from sin and become almost as Christ. "Faith identifies the soul with Christ," Noyes said, "so that by

His death and resurrection the believer dies and rises again, not literally, nor yet figuratively, but spiritually; and thus, so far as sin is concerned, is placed beyond the grave, in heavenly places with Christ."

Noyes was only carrying to an extreme the most important religious idea of the day—that God was closer to the heart of man than earlier generations of Americans had believed. The sense of the immediate presence of God, fostered by revivals since the Second Great Awakening, preached by new theologians, and felt by thousands of the common people, set the reformers' souls aflame. Given the power of God and the ability of man to do his will, surely reform did not await some distant day for victory. "Already a host is coming up to the help of the Lord against the mighty," William Lloyd Garrison announced in 1833, "and the prospect before us is full of encouragement." The watchwords of the abolitionists in the 1830s were "immediate abolition." Although the phrase was not new, although it had different interpretations, it meant that the abolitionists had rejected the old emphasis on gradualism, had rejected everything that smacked of temporizing with evil. Immediatism, David Brion Davis wrote, expressed an "inner freedom, or moral sincerity and earnestness, and . . . victory over selfish and calculating expediency." With the new moral sincerity, victory was surely not afar. In 1828 the American Peace Society's magazine, the *Harbinger,* argued that the end of centuries of human warfare might well be imminent: "The thing is not impossible. *It depends on us.* An union of action among all the Christians and philanthropists of the day would surely accomplish it, so far as Christendom is concerned, provided the present favorable crisis be seized, and no war should break out to blast our prospects, before our principles come into operation, for there is no moral difficulty which zeal and perseverance will not overcome—there is nothing that ought to be done which zeal and intelligence will not do." At exactly the same time the officers of the American Society for the Promotion of Temperance were joyfully predicting a speedy and complete rout of the Demon Rum. And what was it but a sense of immediate and total victory over literally everything that led William Miller and the Millerites to anticipate Christ's Second Advent in 1843—and then in the spring of 1844, and then in the fall?

For better or worse, the Second Advent never came, and the Millerites came away from their millennial expectations sadder, though not necessarily wiser, men. Except for the abolitionists, the ultimate triumph eluded all the reformers. They found progress but not success; they made great numbers of converts but never enough. By 1860 reform was surely not dead—though it was less vigorous than it had been in the 1830s—but most reformers had lost their conviction of impending victory. Yet optimism nourished antebellum reform in its beginnings and sustained the reformers through persecution and suffering and—this above all—gave the reformers together after 1830 an urgency and a force, an enthusiasm and a zeal, which most reformers of earlier years had lacked.

The most important aspect of antebellum reform, however, was that the most important of all the reforms concerned the nature and meaning of the American nation itself. In several ways abolitionism and the southern reaction against it opened questions about the essence of American democracy and its institutions. From the abolitionist viewpoint Negro slavery was anathema to Christian principles, to natural law and natural rights, to the tenets of democracy embodied in the Constitution. While slavery lasted, the United States was in league with sin, horribly imperfect, a stench in the nostrils of God and man. But while the abolitionists fumed at slavery and slaveholders, while they pleaded with the people to help purify the nation and make the dream of freedom a reality, southerners saw different issues at stake. The most obvious one was the question of the rights of the minority in a government of majority rule. Through the states' rights and proslavery arguments southerners sought to protect what they claimed as their natural and Constitutional right to own slaves, their natural and Constitutional right to determine their domestic institutions and ways of life for themselves. But pervading the proslavery argument was a more fundamental and far more difficult question, upon whose answer abolitionists and proslaveryites could never agree. Both groups did agree that they should follow natural law, Christian principles, and Constitutional mandates. They could never agree, however, on who should have the right, and who should have the power, to define those things. Whatever Americans of the day believed were the laws and rights which Nature bestowed upon men, for example, it is clear to the historian that natural law and natural rights had no objective, inherent meaning. The Americans interpreted them as time and circumstance and personality decreed. Thus the most significant right was the right *to define* natural rights for oneself. The American political system provided no means whatever for deciding in whose hands that most important of all rights should lie.

Nor did the United States possess any means whatever for settling moral disputes of great moment. The question of slavery was always a moral question—of whether the institution was right or wrong, of whether northerners or southerners should have the right to decide which it was. Even when slavery seemed most a political problem, as it did in the 1850s, the moral aspect of the dispute over it was always fundamental. Stanley M. Elkins, in *Slavery,* has argued brilliantly that the absence of effective institutions for settling the slavery dispute was a national disaster. The "great falling-short in American society," Elkins said, "was precisely its lack of proper channels for the launching either of its passion or its moderation, either of its propaganda, its slogan-making, or its deepest counsels of understanding." The abolitionists' wrath at slavery and slaveholders, their constant refreshment at the wells of vitriol, were the result of their estrangement from southerners; their sense of personal and national guilt was the greater because there were no established institutions through which they could work and through whose work they could feel that they were moving toward victory. There were no institutions, either, which might have tempered the propaganda, which might have allowed moralists from both sections to make a start at resolving their differences. There was, Elkins pointed out, no national church, no national university, no national "focus of social and financial power," no national bar, no "seaboard social axis stretching from Boston to Charleston, whose vested loyalties might have gone deeper than local ones." Had such institutions existed, Elkins suggested, they might well have staved off the violence of war. The Civil War, of course, did solve the problem of slavery once and for all. But the Civil War was clear proof that American democracy had utterly failed to create means to solve moral problems peaceably. The so-called "compromises" of 1820, 1833, and 1850 were compromises only of the political expressions of moral differences. Moral questions are always the most important questions that men or nations can face; in 1861 the United States and its sections confessed their inability to deal with them by going to war.

PRAYER AND PERSUASION

Fortunately for the nation's peace, and for its citizens' lives and limbs, most of the antebellum reformers rejected violence as a means of change. In general the reformers used four methods to gain their goals: prayers to God, persuasion, example, and coercion through law. Pray and pray again to help the slaves, Harriet Beecher Stowe told the readers of *Uncle Tom's Cabin*. "Do you believe in prayer?" she asked, "or has it become an indistinct apostolic tradition? You pray for the heathen abroad; pray also for the heathen at home. And pray also for those distressed Christians whose sole chance of religious improvement is an accident of trade and sale; from whom any adherence to the morals of Christianity is, in many cases, an impossibility, unless they have given them, from above, the courage and grace of martyrdom." Prayer had *"power with God,"* said one of the American Tract Society's pamphlets. "There is not in the universe a being who, compared with God, has any susceptibility to the influence of prayer. What emanations of love has it drawn from his heart! What blessings of goodness from his hand! His mightiest acts have been achieved in answer to prayer. 'What terrible judgments have been averted; what mighty armies conquered; nay, more, the very course of nature changed—the sun himself arrested—by the power of prayer!' Who can assign the limits of that power? Who can tell what influence prayer has had on the government of God in this world?"

Who indeed could tell? One thing that every God-oriented reformer knew, however, was that the Almighty had not the slightest intention of eliminating wrong and establishing virtue through a miracle or in an instant. God might move in many devious ways His wonders to perform, but His way was not to set aside natural law or even human institutions to work His will. Instead He relied on the work of men. Thousands of reformers believed that God's spirit worked through them and their activities, that through their agency God was at work to expand their causes, to make converts to Christ and to reform, to sustain them when the going was hard. More often than they prayed for immediate and final triumph, they asked for the strength to continue and increase their efforts, for "assurance in the right," as Abraham Lincoln, the reformer-as-President, would say in 1865, "as God gives us to see the right." Whether God was actually working His will through the reformers was anybody's guess. But many a reformer thought He was, and that was what counted.

Obviously the Creator was unwilling to change men's hearts unless the reformers helped. Through incredible quantities of persuasive propaganda the reformers labored to convince their fellow citizens that they should cast off old lives for new and, more than that, join the reform host. The literature of reform taken collectively appealed to every human interest and emotion that ingenious reformers could conceive. In a Protestant nation, first, they had to convince men that their wrongdoing was an abomination in God's sight. Reformers squeezed their Bibles dry to prove that slavery was wrong—the best collection of arguments was Theodore Dwight Weld's *The Bible against Slavery* (New York, 1838)—that the Almighty detested alcohol, whether fermented or distilled, that pacifism was God's way, that educational institutions were necessary to help youths understand God's moral and natural laws, that Roman Catholics were minions of Satan. Dorothea Dix claimed that lifting the burden of misery from the insane was a "sacred cause." Louis Dwight, leader of the Boston Prison Discipline Society, argued that prisons should be places for reforming criminals, rather than merely for punishing or detaining them, and asserted that reformation was what God desired. After all, Dwight contended, criminals were also "creatures of the same glorious Creator with ourselves." They, too, had immortal souls, and were "objects of regard to Christ. . . . The very aggravation of their guilt is the loud call for your pity and prayers, and efforts." Within the prisons, as W. David Lewis has shown in his excellent *From Newgate to Dannemora: The Rise of the Penitentiary in New York, 1796-1848* (Ithaca, 1965), many a warden tried to make the vision of God's love and a respect for His commandments motivations for personal reform.

The God-oriented reformers believed that love of the Creator and love of His creatures were but opposite sides of the same gold coin of righteousness. There were no arbitrary distinctions to be drawn between religious reform and humanitarianism. To do the work of God, the reformers said, was to make men happier on earth; to make men happier on earth was to do the work of God. Not to help in the crusade for more schools of higher quality, Horace Mann contended in 1842, was to sin alike against God and man. As fervently as any religious revivalist, Mann said that the nation was suffering all sorts of evils that education would help to eradicate. There were "innumerable sufferings" which sprang from ignorance, and multitudes "tormented with unnecessary and gratuitous pain," whom education could help. There were "ten thousand existing causes of misery and crime" that education could remove. "Save, O, save the myriads of innocent beings who are just landing on the shores of time;—save them from the contaminations of the world into which they are sent; teach not their unpolluted lips to utter curses, nor their hands to uphold injustice, nor their feet to wander in forbidden paths." God would one day demand an accounting from every man of his stewardship to help children know Him better, Mann said, and fulfilling that stewardship would make both God and men happier.

Happiness, the reformers knew very well, meant different things to different men. For some it meant a release from sin, for others—the slaves, the insane—a freedom from bodily suffering, for still others greater material prosperity. Leading pacifists, Merle E. Curti showed in *The American Peace Crusade, 1815-1860* (Durham, 1929), were fond of pointing out how much money war cost men and nations, how much more prosperous peace would make them. The abolitionists tried to show that slavery was costly to both southerners and the nation at large; the women's rights leaders were seeking, among many other things, power for married women to own property; labor union leaders were interested in better working conditions and higher pay; and the various forms of socialism promised material as well as moral happiness if only men would forsake their present modes of production, distribution, and, above all, competition. Much of the temperance propaganda was designed to prove that drinking cost men not only their physical health, their family happiness, and their personal honor, but also their jobs and savings. Temperance, by contrast, was a happy, moneymaking way of life. Behold the decay of the promising man who took to drink, the Reverend Jonathan Kittredge said in his "Address on the Effects of Ardent Spirits." Once, while a teetotaler, he had an "active, enterprising mind," and he grew up with "every prospect of usefulness." He entered into business, prospered, accumulated property, and was well on his way to financial independence. He married and sired children, and "all was prosperous and happy around him." But then—for reasons Kittredge did not explain—he fell in with the Demon Rum. The results were frightful:

He was seen at the store and the tavern. By degrees he became intemperate. He neglected his business, and his affairs went to gradual decay. He is now a drunkard, his property is wasted, his parents have died of broken hearts, his wife is pale and emaciated, his children ragged, and squalid, and ignorant. He is the tenant of some little cabin that poverty has erected to house him from the storm and the tempest. He is useless, and worse than useless: he is a pest to all around him. All the feelings of his nature are blunted; he has lost all shame; he procures his accustomed supply of the poison that consumes him; he staggers through mud and through filth to his hut; he meets a weeping wife and starving children; he abuses them, he tumbles into his straw, and he rolls and foams like a mad brute, till he is able to go again. He calls for more rum—he repeats the scene from time to time, and from day to day, till soon his nature faints, and he becomes sober in death.

In its way Kittredge's imaginative portrayal had caught not only the economic motivation present in so much of the reform literature, but a number of other motivations as well. It appealed alike to the wrongdoer's self-respect; to self-pity in the drinker and an altruistic pity in the present and prospective temperance reformers; to fear and horror; to wrath against liquor itself and, by a slight extension, to those who made it available. Kittredge and his fellow reformers, moreover, knew very well that while erroneous or evil ideas had to dwell in the minds of individuals, the erroneous or evil things they did as the result of holding those ideas had important social consequences.

The problem of the relation between the reformation of individuals and the reformation of society has troubled historians. As a group they have divided antebellum reform into several categories, which are often more confusing than enlightening. There allegedly existed "individual" and "social," "institutional" and "moral" reform. (There was also "philanthropic" and "charity" and "benevolent" and "religious" reform. And there was "liberal," "progressive," "conservative," "political," and "economic" reform.) "Reform in pre-Civil War America," Louis Filler wrote perplexingly in *A Dictionary of American Social Reform,* "divided into political reform, led by the Jacksonians . . . , and the moral reform of abolitionists, temperance, women's rights, and other advocates." The reform sponsored by political parties, Filler said, was often "symbolic or demagogic," as it was with the Jacksonians. It was Andrew Jackson's contempt for Negroes and Indians, Filler argued, that distinguished him from the moral reformers. For whereas reform itself was in large degree a "process of adjusting outmoded circumstances to more modern wants," moral reform added a "component of principle to reform," and involved a "search for more permanent values, as well as a regard for the possibility of eternal principles of justice. Moral reform is often the dynamo behind practical reform." Filler's differentiations were not easy to understand, but he was not alone in his difficulties of grappling with the distinctions between various kinds of reform. John R. Bodo said in *The Protestant Clergy and Public Issues, 1812-1848* that the differences between moral reform and social reform was that moral reform concerned the reformation of individuals, whereas social reform was a change in social institutions so that individuals might have better lives. If the distinction seemed valid, when compared with Louis Filler's ideas, it threw the reader into confusion. For where Filler believed that both abolitionism and the women's rights movement were moral reforms, Bodo said specifically that abolitionism and the women's rights movement were social reforms. If the reader wanted to confuse himself the more, he could throw into the discussion an observation that Richard Hofstadter made in an essay on Wendell Phillips in *The American Political Tradition and the Men Who*

Made It (New York, 1948). As an abolitionist, Phillips was a moral reformer according to Filler, and a social reformer according to Bodo. Hofstadter thought Phillips an "agitator"—that is, a reformer—whose work it was to "influence the public mind in the interest of some large social transformation."

Now it was true that there were distinctions and differences in antebellum reform and in reform propaganda. The temperance reformer who labored to get drunkards to sign the pledge of total abstinence to save themselves from sin and death was clearly doing something different from the founders of Brook Farm who were replacing undesirable social institutions with cooperative institutions that seemed to promise more. In 1849 the officers of the American Sunday School Union of Philadelphia said that "Instead of making the invisible, intangible and irresponsible condition we call SOCIETY the scape-goat for the sins and sufferings of the visible, tangible and responsible individuals who compose it . . . we should . . . hold the individuals to answer for the burdens and griefs of society." To an anarchist like Josiah Warren, however, such an idea was preposterous. Although individuals certainly played some role in producing misery for themselves and society, institutions played a far greater role. They enforced conformity; they deprived people of their personal uniqueness and independence—the "Sovereignty of the Individual" was Warren's motto and his goal; they were an evil curse which had to be lifted. Governments generally, Warren wrote in 1852, had only

spread wholesale destruction, famine, and wretchedness, in every frightful form over all parts of the earth, where peace and security might otherwise have prevailed. They have shed more blood, committed more murders, tortures, and other frightful crimes in the struggles against each other *for the privilege of governing,* than society ever would or could have suffered in the total absence of all governments whatever! . . . They invade the private household, they impertinently meddle with, and in their blind and besotted wantonness, presume to regulate the most sacred individual feelings. . . . They set up rules or laws to which they require conformity, while conformity

is impossible, and while neither rulers nor ruled can tell how the laws will be interpreted or administered! Under such circumstances, no security for the governed can exist.

Yet differences in approach were not differences in general objectives. The reformers themselves knew that every moral reformer was also a social reformer, that moral reform *meant* social reform, and that social reform *meant* a moral reformation. The mixture of individual reform and the reform of society characterized all the reform propaganda to the extent that historians' distinctions became almost distortions. In 1843, for example, the Reverend Gardiner Spring of New York, a Presbyterian supporter of almost every moral reform and an officer of several reform societies, wrote that a mass conversion to Christian precepts would save society from its chief threats: "resistance to lawful authority," "clamor about the rights of man," "tumultuous conventions," "arraignment and abuse of the courts of justice," "the bold assumption of the power of the law by an infuriated mob." *"The Gospel is the most economical police on earth,"* said the leaders of the American Home Missionary Society. An American Tract Society agent claimed that when individuals morally reformed themselves they would help to "bridge over the dangerous chasm between the rich and the poor; so that instead of . . . mobs and outbreaks . . . destroying life and property, there will be between these two great classes a reciprocation of confidence and good feeling, as there will be also a ready recognition of their mutual dependence, their harmonious interests, and their immortal brotherhood." Every abolitionist knew that slavery was a sin and that abolitionism was a moral reform; every abolitionist also knew that he was attacking a social and legal institution in order to improve the Negroes' lot and that thereby he was a social reformer. He was a social reformer, too, in that he sought to free all of American society from the guilt for slavery's existence. And what was anti-Catholicism, after all, but a moral reform and a social reform at the same time? To convert Catholics to Protestantism was to help purify American society and protect it from the evil machinations of the institutionalized hierarchy. To stir American Protestants to hate the Church was to help destroy that institution—though anti-Catholics never explained precisely how hatred worked—and thus to make the moral reformation of individuals possible.

In 1840, when Albert Brisbane published *The Social Destiny of Man* (Philadelphia) to convert Americans to the gospel of Charles Fourier, he described his ideas specifically as "social reform." Yet among the advantages of living in the cooperative way, Brisbane said, were that people would become truthful rather than fraudulent in all relations of life, and that collective and individual philanthropy would replace universal selfishness; if these were not moral reforms as both contemporaries and historians have used the term, the term had no meaning at all. In 1841, when George Ripley and his friends wrote a constitution for Brook Farm—it was not at the time a Fourierist phalanx—they made the same point. By replacing bad institutions with good institutions, they said, they intended to promote the "great purposes of human culture," which meant among other things guaranteeing to each other the "means of physical support, and of spiritual progress; and thus to impart a greater freedom, simplicity, truthfulness, refinement, and moral dignity, to our mode of life." Institutional reform, then, was a means of helping the Brook Farmers reform themselves as individuals, as moral agents.

Thus through reform, said the literature, men could improve or perfect both themselves and society. Individual evil was a curse to the individual, to his family and friends, to society at large; the evil of social institutions (government, the economic system, false churches, war, the neighborhood saloon) blighted individual minds, bodies, and moral sensibilities. There *were* enormous differences among the antebellum reformers in fundamental approach. But to try to see some of them as only moral reformers and others as only social reformers hid more light than it shed.

Brook Farm itself, along with several dozen other Fourierist phalanxes that sprang up in the 1840s, along with John Humphrey Noyes's Oneida Community, were efforts at reform through example. The reformers generally were always delighted when they could exhibit themselves or others as men who had once lived improperly or unhappily, had seen the light, and were now enjoying the consequences. It was one thing to tell men that they ought to change their lives and their institutions, to describe to them the beneficial results of change. It was another thing— another kind of persuasion—to offer an actual communitarian society in operation, to exhibit a person whom love had helped or an actual former drunkard who had made something of himself after he signed the pledge. John Humphrey Noyes could have preached perfectionism and the need for communal living forever without achieving a hundredth of the effect that the creation and maintenance of his Oneida Community had. The community's success, indeed, strengthened Noyes's own certainty, as he said in 1867, that socialism based on religious grounds was a "true principle and one that is dear to the heavens . . . and I expect that this principle and not Republicanism, (the mere power of human law), will at last triumph in some form here and throughout the world." In the 1820s and 1830s temperance lecturers hauled reformed drunkards up on the platform whenever they could find them; in the 1840s, after the start of the Washingtonian movement, the former topers themselves seized the initiative. The most famous lecturer of the decade was John B. Gough, a frequently inebriated one-time actor who signed the pledge in 1842. A spellbinder on the platform, Gough contrasted his present happiness with his former misery so effectively that a contemporary newspaper account described one of his audiences as "alternately elevated by the grand, thrilled with the horrible, dissolved with the tender, enchanted with the beautiful." So popular was Gough that he survived a personal disaster that would have destroyed a lesser man. On a visit to New York City in 1845, Gough suddenly vanished. After a search his friends found him in a whorehouse apparently recovering from a drunken spree that had lasted for several days. Gough claimed that a chance acquaintance had invited him to have a glass of soda in a drugstore, and that after drinking it he had become dazed, lost his way, and, in some fashion that he could not explain, ended up among the painted ladies. He could not remember if he had followed the soda with liquor. His enemies and even some of his friends were sure that he had fallen off the wagon; if he had, he climbed right back on and continued successfully to make an example of himself.

To extreme idealists, such as Ralph Waldo Emerson in the late 1830s and the 1840s, and to people in whom idealism ran stronger than it did in most others, like Harriet Beecher Stowe, the example of a single person who simply felt right could accomplish enormous amounts of good. If the "single man," Ralph Waldo Emerson said in "The American Scholar" in 1837, would but "plant himself indomitably on his instincts, and there abide, the huge world will come round to him. Patience—patience; with the shades of all the good and great for company; and for solace the perspective of your own infinite life; and for work the study and the communication of principles, the making those instincts prevalent, the conversion of the world." What could northerners do to help Negroes? Mrs. Stowe asked at the end of *Uncle Tom's Cabin*. They could pray, she answered, they could receive fugitive and emancipated slaves into their churches and schools, and "they can see to it that *they feel right*. An atmosphere of sympathetic influence," Mrs. Stowe thought, "encircles every human being; and the man or woman who *feels* strongly, healthily and justly, on the great interests of humanity, is a constant benefactor to the human race. See, then, to your sympathies in this matter! Are they in harmony with the sympathies of Christ? or are they swayed and perverted by the sophistries of worldly policy?"

COERCION

Although the antebellum reformers believed that God answered their prayers by giving them strength, although they knew that their persuasive propaganda and the example they offered did change many men's thoughts and deeds, numbers of reformers knew that prayer, persuasion, and example were not enough. If reformers were originally confident of early victory, they were also extremely impatient, determined to neglect no idea or agency that promised help. For many of them, coercion through law proved at least as attractive as other means, and sometimes more attractive. Such reformers sought to convince local, state, and national legislators that they should impose morality upon sinners and society, that they should further benevolence and philanthropy by legal power.

The relationship between antebellum reform and antebellum politics has perplexed historians for some time. Although most historians now realize that reform had all sorts of political manifestations, a few writers have claimed that reform and political action were different kinds of endeavors. One of the earlier proponents of the distinction was Carl Russell Fish. In 1927, in *The Rise of the Common Man, 1830-1850,* Fish grappled manfully with the problem of defining reform, and came off second best. Saying that reform was a "touchstone which differentiated people more incisively than did party allegiance," and that reform was "something rather felt by instinct than defined by reason," Fish argued that "political reforms" were not reforms at all: they were "regarded as a mere extension and application of principles already accepted and approved. 'Reform' had usually some social implications." Fish's perplexity ran as a kind of minority undercurrent in the mainstream of historical writing. In 1939, for example, Arthur M. Schlesinger, Jr., argued in his biography of *Orestes A. Brownson: A Pilgrim's Progress* (Boston) that "moral" reformers "ignored the relationship between ethical conduct and the social setting." It had never been made clear, Schlesinger wrote, "just how the moral reformers hoped to make man virtuous, and there is their fatal weakness." Reform itself meant "practical attempts to improve conditions," and that in turn meant political legislation instigated by political parties, which excluded the moral reformers. In 1945 Schlesinger made about the same point in *The Age of Jackson* (Boston). Although he said very little about the welter of non-Jacksonian reforms after 1830, Schlesinger asserted that such an important reform movement as utopian socialism was only "pseudo-reform." It was in the arena of party politics that the "battles of reform" were actually fought. Real reform, meaningful reform, was Jacksonian Democracy in action. In 1960 Henry Steele Commager alleged in *The Era of Reform* that "on the whole, reform was not political, and politics was not reformist." Reformers such as Horace Mann and Dorothea Dix, Commager admitted, had to work through the "machinery of the state," but they were the exceptions which proved the generalization. Because the reformers obeyed the higher law of virtue, Commager said, because they believed that government actually supported evils such as wars and slavery and the subordination of women, the reformers were indifferent to politics and positively repudiated politics. They recognized, Commager said, the "futility of reliance on party."

Yet most historians knew very well that a great part of antebellum reform was political, that it relied on politicians and parties for success, that reformers oriented toward politics made no distinction at all between reform and political action. As Commager did point out, some of the antebellum reformers had as their goal a change in existing laws, the better to increase both individual and social happiness. Horace Mann and Dorothea Dix and the women's-righters were obvious examples; in addition there were prison reformers, benevolent men such as Samuel Gridley Howe who wanted improved facilities for the care of the deaf, dumb, and blind, and others who wanted to improve the care given orphans and paupers. It was precisely because governments fought wars that pacifists sought to get Congressional approval of stipulated arbitration treaties and to convince politicians that war was evil. Two of the chief desires of American nativists were that the national government lengthen the period that immigrants have to reside in the United States before they could become citizens— some would have it as long as twenty-one years—and that no immigrant be allowed to vote until he became a naturalized citizen. At the state level nativists constantly urged legislators to pass laws denying recent immigrants the power to vote.

Every reformer who saw some uses for politics, indeed, turned to the coercive power of government for aid. The emphasis on laws as means of reform, moreover, appeared very early in several movements; reformers were so eager for success that they saw no reason to use only the slower processes of persuasion. By 1830 the officers of the American Society for the Promotion of Temperance, organized in 1826, desired that "legislation should exert its appropriate power and influence" to help rescue tipplers and save would-be drinkers. For the next two decades temperance men championed laws to destroy saloons—then called grog-shops —by forbidding the sale of liquor in small quantities, and to give counties, cities, and villages the local option to decide whether liquor could be sold within them. When all else failed, they turned to statewide prohibition of the manufacture and sale of spirits except for medicinal and mechanical purposes. In 1828 various northeastern moralists formed the General Union for Promoting the Observance of the Christian Sabbath, and from its start its main purpose was political. Although the Union organizers hoped to persuade individuals to keep the Sabbath holy by refraining from toil and travel, their greater goal was to induce Congress to pass a law forbidding the transport of the mails on Sunday. The Union's leaders, moreover, were playing a devious political game. While they were convinced moralists, they were also convinced anti-Jacksonians who hoped to embarrass the new President and his Congressional supporters by thrusting the Sunday mails issue upon them. If Congress and the President abolished the Sunday mails, the Sabbatarians had won a victory; if the Sunday mails were not abolished—as they were not—the Sabbatarians could portray their political enemies as immoral men—as they did. Other moral reformers were just as eager to use political institutions for victory. In the late 1830s both the American Sunday School Union and the American Bible Society began efforts to get their publications into and read in the states' common schools. Doing so would both cleanse the children's morals and sell more books. Expressing the beliefs of his fellow zealots, A. Bruyn Hasbrouck, a prominent lawyer from Kingston, New York, told the Bible Society's members that Bible reading in the common schools could not in any way violate freedom of belief or the "rights of conscience. . . . A nation without a Bible is a nation without a conscience," Hasbrouck said scornfully, "and so without the rights of conscience to be violated."

Politics and morality, politics and righteousness, politics and reform were for many reformers one and the same. Especially were they one and the same for great numbers of abolitionists. Most of them thought slavery both a religious sin and a political wrong, and while they strove to make northerners realize and hate the southerners' sins, they also did their utmost to get help from politicians. The American Anti-Slavery Society's Declaration of Sentiments of 1833 conceded that under the Constitution Congress could not interfere with slavery in the states. But Congress did have a right and was "solemnly bound" to suppress the interstate slave trade and to abolish slavery in the territories it controlled. The people of the free states, moreover, were under the "highest obligations" to remove slavery by "moral and political action" as prescribed by the Constitution; this meant they should dissolve all relations between the national government and slavery. From 1836 to 1838 abolitionists mounted an awesome campaign of petitions to Congress. Memorials bearing thousands and then ten thousands of signatures asked Congressmen to abolish slavery in the national territories and the District of Columbia, to refuse admission to new slave states, especially Texas, and to abolish the interstate slave trade. Congress, of course, refused to heed the petitions. Faced with Congressional proslaveryism, or apathy, or fear of offending colleagues and constituents, confronted with so-called "gag rules" by which antislavery petitions were laid on the table rather than referred to committee, the abolitionists turned more zealously than before to electing themselves and their sympathizers to the national legislature. They questioned candidates and tried to force politicians to take a stand on slavery. In 1839 and 1840 several abolitionists formed the Liberty party, an organization designed to draw the votes of antislavery Whigs and Democrats. In 1840 and 1844 the Liberty party's candidate for President was James G. Birney, a former slaveholder who had seen the error of his ways and become an active abolitionist. Not surprisingly, Birney failed both times. But as Betty Fladeland has told well in *James Gillespie Birney: Slaveholder to Abolitionist* (Ithaca, 1955), by 1844 the Liberty party had increased its vote 800 percent (from about 7,000 in 1840 to over 62,000) and had strengthened its organization at the local levels.

Not all the abolitionists, to be sure, were consistent supporters of political action. In the late 1830s William Lloyd Garrison and some loyal followers turned away from politics in despair and disgust. Having once believed that political action would be effective, they came to believe Christian perfectionism a better means. Learning much from John Humphrey Noyes, as John L. Thomas's *The Liberator* explains, Garrison began to preach the gospel of immediate and universal emancipation from sin. He became even more of a visionary than he had been before. The nation's only hope, he said, was for everyone to become as free from evil as Christ had been. Garrison had no explanation for how such personal regeneration would help abolish slavery, but now it was clear that politicians and political parties were of no use at all, that government had nothing to offer the reformer, that reliance on the Liberty party was contrary to the will of God. By 1842 Garrison was calling for a dissolution of the Union, a separation of northern freedom from southern slavery, to preserve the one and abolish the other. If this was political action of a kind, Garrison never made clear how a northern repudiation of the Constitution would end slavery in the southern Union that remained.

But no matter. In the 1840s and 1850s the most important aspect of the antislavery impulse was political. To be sure, nonpolitical moralists continued to damn slavery and slaveholders and the South generally. Their tone became ever shriller as they discovered—or thought they discovered—new evidences of moral callousness in such things as the Mexican War; the debates and contents of the Compromise of 1850; and, later, the Kansas-Nebraska Act and its aftermath in Kansas. But it was in its political forms that antislaveryism affected the nation most. Even as the nation and its politicians tussled with political problems, however—with slavery's expansion into the territories, with fugitive slave laws, with the question of how much power southerners ought to have within the Whig and Democratic parties—none of slavery's political enemies ever forgot that slavery was a moral wrong; a cruel sin; a violation of God's will, of natural law, of decency and humanity. When men such as Joshua Giddings, Salmon P. Chase, and Benjamin F. Wade of Ohio, or George W. Julian of Indiana, or Charles Sumner and Henry Wilson of Massachusetts rose in Congress to condemn southern political machinations, they spoke as moral reformers. Thus on February 21, 1854, when Charles Sumner demanded that the Senate refuse to repeal the Missouri Compromise, which repeal was now part of the bill to organize the Nebraska Territory, he reminded his listeners on the floor and in the galleries of the nature of slavery itself.

Slavery is the forcible subjection of one human being, in person, labor, and property, to the will of another. In this simple statement is involved its whole injustice. There is no offence against religion, against morals, against humanity, which, in the license of this enormity, may not stalk "unwhipped of justice." For the husband and wife there is no marriage; for the mother there is no assurance that her infant child will not be ravished from her breast; for all who bear the name of Slave there is nothing that they can call their own. Without a father, without a mother, almost without a God, the slave has nothing but a master. It would be contrary to that Rule of Right which is ordained by God, if such a system, though mitigated often by patriarchal kindness, and by plausible physical comfort, could be otherwise than pernicious. It is confessed that the master suffers not less than the slave. And this is not all. The whole social fabric is disorganized; labor loses its dignity; industry sickens; education finds no schools; and all the land of Slavery is impoverished.

In one form or another abolitionists had been saying precisely the same things for generations, and the new abolitionists had been trying to sear the souls of northerners with such statements for a quarter-century. Political action was another way of working for God, for man, for morality, for happiness, for the nation—for everything, in short, that reformers had always claimed to work.

There was, then, no single pattern to antebellum reform. Variety was its theme and pluralism its nature. There was no single spirit of reform and no single means of accomplishing it. Nor was there any single way to assess the consequences of reform upon either the antebellum United States or the United States of a later day.

THREE

The Consequences of Reform

THE ROOTS OF FAILURE

Ralph Waldo Emerson, seer that he was, knew very well that most reformers would fail to win any final triumph over evil and pain. They would fail, that is, unless they reformed themselves and their methods first. In his "Lecture on the Times," delivered in Boston in December, 1841, he said that the reformers' means were inadequate to reach their goals. The reformers foolishly relied for victory on institutions, politics, churches, other men, "circumstances" generally. All those things were useless and lifeless. By "combination of that which is dead," Emerson said, "they hope to make something alive. In vain." The only thing that could remake man was "new infusions" of the spirit of God, of that spirit which made and directed man himself. Earlier that year, speaking before the Boston Mechanics' Apprentices' Library Association, Emerson had urged every man to become a reformer. "What is a man born for but to be a Reformer," he asked, "a Re-maker of what man has made; a renouncer of lies; a restorer of truth and good . . . ?" But the true means of reform, he warned his audience, was universal love, the love which came directly from God and before whose force nothing but love could stand. Love would creep where force could never go; love could accomplish what force could never achieve. In "application to great interests" love was now "obsolete and forgotten," even though this "great, overgrown, dead Christendom of ours still keeps alive at least the name of a lover of mankind. But one day all men will be lovers; and every calamity will be dissolved in the universal sunshine."

That day never came. Emerson himself was among the greatest failures of all the reformers. Only a handful of Americans ever shared his transcendentalist ideals and vision and universal love. As an analyst and prophet of the reformers and their future, however, he was superb. Whether love would have won final victories over the nation's calamities was, of course, questionable; in any case, love's full power remained to be tested. Whatever love the antebellum reformers had, or professed to have, for their fellow men, however, they continued to rely for success on traditional means. As a result they made progress. But also as a result by 1860 no reformer had accomplished all that he had set out to do. During the next five years, to be sure, abolitionists would succeed in ending slavery in the United States. Yet in a curious way the abolitionists' use of the Civil War to destroy Negro bondage was the strongest evidence, the most obvious token, of their peculiar failure by 1860, the last year of peace. That failure joined them with the other reformers, who would have no such success in the years ahead. During the preceding thirty years the reformers as a group had claimed that victory was possible without violent social up-heaval, without revolution, without bloodshed. If there were some violent spirits among the reformers, most of them had no desire to overthrow evil institutions by armed force or to execute the evildoers who stood between them and triumph. Great numbers of reformers did hope to use the power of the state to impose re-forms upon a recalcitrant people, but even these reformers worked well within the accepted political ways. Until the Civil War, which was certainly a radical departure from previous experience, no group of reformers succeeded completely, and no reformer could be sure of maintaining his progress or holding the ground he had won. As welcome as progress and partial victories were, they were measures of how much more remained to be done, keen reminders of the continuing grasp of wrong ideas on the Americans' minds.

A century later there was no single way, and no simple way, either, to account for the successes and failures of all the various reform movements. By the mid-1960s there was no general study of antebellum reform which explained the reasons for the relative popularity of different reforms, for the varying rates of progress the reformers made, for their greater or lesser impacts upon American society. Antebellum reform as a whole, and the reformers all together, were subjects which badly needed comprehensive, synthesizing study. But on the basis of the large number of recent monographs and biographies, some tentative generalizations and several hypotheses are possible.

Curiously enough, the conditions of American life which pro-duced and sustained the welter of reforms also prevented any one of them from being entirely successful. In antebellum America any cause short of a violent overthrow of all existing institutions could find a hearing and at least a few sympathizers. The diversity of the American people—in thought and emotion, in will and desire, in present circumstances and dreams of the future—guaranteed a diversity of reforms. In a sense the United States *had* to have its anarchists and its Mormons, its champions of free love and its champions of Sylvester Graham's bread, its bloomer enthusiasts and spiritualists and phrenologists, its abolitionists, anti-Catholics, women's-righters, religious revivalists, and all the rest. The United States, in the same way, *had* to have its benevolent, sweet-souled reformers like William Ellery Channing, and at the opposite extreme its crazed, apocalyptic, wrathful reformers like Nat Turner and John Brown of Harpers Ferry. Every American reformer knew that somewhere, sometime, he could find at least one other heart which beat as his, one other soul which vibrated as his own. In an open society into which men and women of every nature and description were coming, the presence of almost every nature and description of reform was inevitable.

Yet the very diversity of American life and American reform movements prevented any one reform from capturing overwhelming public support. Like the American economy, antebellum reform worked on the free enterprise system. The purveyors of new nostrums for individual and societal ills had to hawk them in the marketplace of ideas. When they entered the marketplace, they found a multitude of other reformers already there, each of them claiming not only that his patent medicine would cure the sickness he fought, but that that particular sickness was the greatest malady men suffered. "Should we specify *one particular vice,*" said the officers of the American Society for the Promotion of Temperance, *"which seems to us most prevalent, most threatening, and most ruinous to the bodies and souls of men; we should say, it is* INTEMPERANCE." Not at all, said the Garrisonian abolitionists. It was slavery that was the "deadliest curse" in the land, the "foulest stain which rests upon our national escutcheon." But every religious revivalist knew that the nation's greatest shame was not the presence of any particular evil, but the more general, and more pervasive, sinfulness caused by men's separation from Christ. Naturally enough the buying public shopped from stall to stall.

They found some reforms more attractive than others, of course, but the variety of reforms made it impossible for any one of them to corner the market. To make matters even more difficult for the reformers, they had to compete for the public interest with a tremendous variety of other excitements and concerns which America offered: the struggles and squabbles of politicians and their parties, the conquering of the West, the search for ever greater wealth, the diversions and alarms of seething cities. By 1861 the only reform movement able to win majority support was the new movement to destroy forever the ideas and work of southern secessionists. And the reason for the support given that movement, as Hans Kohn's *American Nationalism: An Interpretative Essay* (New York, 1957) suggested, was that Americans believed the Union's preservation absolutely necessary to the realization of all men's hopes.

Whatever progress the reformers made, then, depended on what the people generally would accept. Relative successes and failures bore no relation whatever to the intrinsic worth of any reform, or to a reformer's sincerity and earnestness of purpose. Progress and regress rested upon the people's own ideas and the people's own feelings about what they needed. Like any peddler or producer, the reformer could stimulate a demand for his product by advertising. But prosperity came only as his message aroused some predisposition to heed it, and to buy. It was those predispositions of thought and feeling which determined the relative popularity of the various reforms, which made some of them vigorous and others weak.

To understand a reformer's message, people had to relate it in ways both intellectual and emotional to themselves and their environment. They had to appreciate the problem as keenly and to welcome the reformer's cure as heartily as did the reformer himself. Meaningful proposals could not far transcend the present limits of experience and belief, could not be irrelevant to men's actual secular and spiritual concerns. To begin with, a reformer's message had simply to be intelligible to a largely untutored people. The transcendentalists, for example, found that merely communicating their profoundest ideas to the public was difficult. Ralph Waldo Emerson was one of the most popular lecturers of his day, but when he spoke on subjects dearest to his heart, few people could even understand what his words meant. The reason was, as he confessed in "The Oversoul" in 1841, that he was trying to convey the results of his feelings, his intuitions, his ecstasies, his limitless spiritual exaltation; and the words of men were unable to express all that he felt. Trying to describe the spirit of God that pervaded the universe and everything in it, Emerson said that only by yielding to the "spirit of prophecy which is innate in every man" could one understand the unity of all things in the essence of God. "Every man's words who speaks from that life," Emerson wrote, "must sound vain to those who do not dwell in the same thought on their own part. I dare not speak for it. My words do not carry its august sense; they fall short and cold. Only itself can inspire whom it will, and behold! their speech shall be lyrical, and sweet, and universal as the rising of the wind." For the rest of his life Emerson struggled unsuccessfully to find an adequate verbal means of conveying the infinite sublimity of God's infinite spirit. When Emerson spoke or wrote on a specific subject, his language could be most clear and precise. But when he tried to describe to ordinary mortals the splendor of the Creator's essence in Himself and man and nature alike, the mortals knew that they were in the presence of a man of majesty, but they understood him not. The people who heard a religious zealot like Charles Grandison Finney, by contrast, knew exactly what he meant. Finney spoke directly to them in simple language, which was the more powerful as it was the more vulgar. When he told a sinner that he was so evil that if he could climb to heaven he would literally hurl God from His throne and then actually cut God's throat—"Yes, you would cut God's throat!"— the sinner had no trouble at all seeing how wicked Finney thought him. When Finney, along with many another revivalist, pictured the burning lake of hell filled with scalding wretches groaning and screaming, his audiences got the message at once.

Most of the reformers, be it said, did not suffer Emerson's problem. If they could not always convince their readers and listeners, if there were some difficulties in grasping the complexities of, say, John Humphrey Noyes's perfectionism, the reformers generally could make themselves understood. But mere communication of words and ideas did not make a particular reform meaningful. If a reformer demanded changes which passed far beyond the tolerable limits of existing thought and present institutions, if he was committed to some utopia whose ways were radically different from those accepted as good by most people, his chances of success were slight. The reformers who had the grandest and most comprehensive dreams of individual and social reconstruction made the least progress and sustained the greatest defeats. For the transcendentalists, for the communitarian socialists like Noyes and Albert Brisbane and George Ripley, for anarchists like Josiah Warren and Stephen Pearl Andrews, the abyss between desire and accomplishment was wider and deeper than for most other reformers. The transcendentalists, offering men ideas that would allegedly liberate them from grief and oppression of every kind, made few converts. When Brook Farm's great central building, or phalanstery, burned down in 1846, wasting the money that Ripley, Brisbane, and their followers had begged and borrowed, the community had to break up. There was no more money—that is, not enough support from society at large—to continue. In 1851 Josiah Warren and Stephen Pearl Andrews began Modern Times, a community of anarchists on Long Island, and a few years later Modern Times was thriving. But the community attracted all kinds of cranks, and the cranks stirred several New York newspapers—most notably Horace Greeley's reformist *Tribune*—to bitter opposition. The financial panic of 1857 ruined Modern Times, and during the Civil War most of the anarchists who had stuck it out sold their property to men with conventional ideas, and left. The most successful of the utopia builders was John Humphrey Noyes. After the mid-1850s his Oneida Community prospered and grew, largely as the result of Noyes's business acumen and the warmth of personality and strength of purpose that he offered as examples to the members. Yet the great goal of the Oneida leaders was not merely to create a single happy community, but to convert the world—or at least the United States—to socialism and Christian perfectionism. Like other kinds of utopian radicals, they failed.

They failed because the condemnation they made of existing ideas and institutions and the reforms they proposed had no meaning to most of their fellow citizens. The utopian radicals called not merely for partial changes or limited reforms within the existing American order, but for the replacement of present institutions— the churches, the state, the family, the competitive economic system —with allegedly better institutions. They were radicals in the true sense of the word: men and women who dug to the roots of American society, found those roots twisted and diseased, and proposed to pull them up in order to destroy the ugly plants they nourished. In place of root and plant alike they sowed the seeds of other ideas, other institutions whose exotic flowers they thought more beautiful. But the great majority of Americans thought the flowers too exotic. Most men everywhere, after all, have always had trouble even understanding ways of life other than their own. It is much more difficult for them to visualize themselves actually living under very different institutions and thinking new thoughts about a variety of subjects.

It was not merely such innate conservatism, however, that made the utopian radicals fail. For the institutions they proposed to replace were wrong only in their own eyes. Most Americans be- lieved that Constitutional democracy, capitalism, and the numerous Christian churches and their creeds were exactly what the people needed to realize all their own fervent hopes for ever-growing happiness: for ever-greater prosperity, progress, freedom, virtue. Much of popular thought and rhetoric were imbued with a utopian spirit of their own—with a belief that as America's future unfolded the genius of its institutions and its people would make all good dreams, no matter how extravagant, come true. If existing institutions did not work perfectly, there were certainly enough nonradical, nonutopian reformers around to improve them. What was the point of becoming an anarchist in a country where individual freedom was a reality, and where Jacksonian Democratic spokesmen constantly promised to increase its scope? What was the point of becoming a socialist in a land where the opportunities for getting richer were so abundant, and where Jacksonians, Whigs, and Republicans alike promised all sorts of help in grasping those opportunities? More important, what was the point of becoming any kind of utopian radical at a time when the full potentialities of America were still unexplored, when the future was still open, when limited reforms might make existing institutions work as perfectly in practice as they did in theory?

The Reverend Adin Ballou, founder of the Hopedale Community in Massachusetts, spoke for all the utopian radicals when he declared that the Americans were not yet ready for fundamental departures from accepted ways. Hopedale, begun in 1841, was an experiment in Christian socialism, a cooperative, joint-stock enterprise dedicated to all kinds of reform. A prospectus of 1851 described it as a "universal religious, moral, philanthropic, and social reform Association," and a missionary society, a temperance society, an antislavery society, a peace society, and a women's rights association to boot. After a period of great prosperity Hopedale came to an end in the 1850s as the result of the work of two conniving brothers, Ebenezer and George Draper. The Drapers cornered the stock, repudiated the Christian socialism of Ballou and his followers, and gave the Hopedale property over to private enterprise. Looking back on the Hopedale failure in the 1890s, Ballou said that in earlier years the people were not ready for radical changes—nor were they ready now. "The work of Social Reform," he said, "is by no means abandoned; it is only suspended till the world is fitted by intellectual growth and spiritual elevation to take it up again and prosecute it to successful results." If the intellectual and spiritual elevation of the American people in the antebellum years was impressive, it fell far short of the ethereal realms occupied by Ballou and his peers.

SUCCESSES AND SATISFACTIONS

Reformers with far more familiar and far more limited objectives were almost as meaningful as the utopian radicals were meaningless. Measured by any standards, the most successful of the antebellum reform movements were temperance and nativism. Between 1851 and 1855 a Maine Law movement for prohibiting the manufacture and sale of spirituous liquors swept the North and even entered the South. State after state—all New England together with New York, Delaware, Indiana, Iowa, and Michigan —passed Maine Laws of their own; Ohio and Pennsylvania sharply restricted liquor selling; in New Jersey, Maryland, and Wisconsin the Maine Law men missed victory by only a hair. Southern support for the Maine Law grew steadily. At the same time the national nativist lodge, known formally as the Order of the Star-Spangled Banner and organized in 1849, was receiving members by the thousands and entering politics in every state as the American or Know-Nothing party. In the elections of 1854 and 1855 the Know-Nothings carried Massachusetts, Rhode Island, New Hampshire, Connecticut, Delaware, Maryland and Kentucky; in combination with the Whigs, they carried Pennsylvania. They elected most state officers in New York, Pennsylvania, and California; very nearly carried Virginia, Georgia, Alabama, Mississippi, and Louisiana; and held the balance of power in Wisconsin. So great had the nativist cause become that Henry Wilson of Massachusetts, a Know-Nothing Congressman, predicted that the party would win 1,250,000 votes in the presidential elections of 1856, and the New York *Herald* thought it could capture the presidency.

The power of the Maine Law movement and nativism in the 1850s was not only the result of their popularity among the people at large. At the time they had unprecedented support by local and national politicians. The 1850s were a decade of rapid and basic change in the nation's party system. The Whig and Democratic parties were splintering internally as party members argued with each other over several questions: over internal improvements, over the nature of slavery and the desirability of fugitive slave laws and slavery's expansion into the territories, over the best means of winning political power, over which party faction should prevail. Although intraparty fights were nothing new, they were now more bitter than before. In state after state politicians who were seeking new bases of power and politicians who were even looking for a new party, which promised them opportunities that the older parties could not provide, joined to support temperance and nativist principles. Starting in 1854, with the Kansas-Nebraska Act on its way to passage, many of these politicians would add anti-slaveryism and antisouthernism to the other two reforms, and from the increased ferment of reform would come the Republican party.

Yet politicians supported prohibition and nativism because those causes had widespread popularity. The reasons so many Americans backed them, in turn, were that the ideas upon which they rested were thoroughly familiar, and that the evils they attacked were so pressing. As John A. Krout pointed out in *The Origins of Prohibition* (New York, 1925), thousands of Protestant moralists had long described drunkenness—though not drinking —as a sin. Through both preaching and laws the colonies and states had sought to check it. As Ray Allen Billington demonstrated in *The Protestant Crusade,* a good Protestant in the colonial and early national periods had to be something of an anti-Catholic. What was Protestantism, anyway, but a protest against the alleged evil and corruption of the Roman Church in the name of a pure Christianity? Although anti-Catholic sentiment was of slight consequence around 1820—there were few Catholics in the United

States, they had very little power, and the American people had better things to do than to persecute them—Americans still believed Catholicism wrong and Protestantism right. From the 1820s on anti-Catholics and antiliquor reformers could build their crusades on familiar ideas and familiar prejudices; their notions were meaningful to Americans precisely because they were trite.

A cluster of ideas required more than mere familiarity, however, to spur people to act. Even though many Americans thought drunkenness a curse and Catholicism a sin, no widespread reform movements would appear to oppose them unless their existence and the problems they caused were obvious and sizable to people already disposed to hate them. If a reform movement was to be popular, the sickness as well as the cure had to be evident. Unlike the radical utopians, the leaders of the temperance and anti-Catholic crusades found sickness all about them, and their followers saw it just as clearly. By 1810 a nation of some 7,200,000 people already had an estimated 14,191 distilleries producing over 25,000,-000 gallons of spirits a year; there were certainly additional hundreds of family stills in the rural districts. Then and in the years ahead all a man had to do to see the effects of liquor was to rove the streets of his city or town, read his newspaper, or reflect back on his own drunken sprees. Drunkenness bred observable crime and violence and misery and a contempt of the lower classes for their social and moral superiors—as their social and moral superiors knew very well from personal experience. From local discontents and local temperance and moral reform societies, a national movement was bound to emerge. No one man got it going, but the greatest temperance advocate of the 1820s was the Reverend Lyman Beecher, pastor of the Congregational church in Litchfield, Connecticut, and one of the most eminent divines of his day. In the fall of 1825 Beecher preached a series of six sermons on intemperance. Printed and reprinted by the thousands in the years to come, they argued not only that intemperance was growing at a fearful rate, but that the way to end intemperance was to abolish liquor itself from the land. Beecher was preaching ideas which had been growing in popularity of late among temperance men: that drunkenness was the inevitable result of drinking, that only total abstinence could end intemperance. The latter idea did separate the new temperance movement from the old. But the intemperance problem was so great, and mere pleas for temperate drinking had so clearly failed to end drunkenness, that it made good sense, and it was a departure in means only, not in ends. From arguments for total abstinence to demands for prohibition, moreover, was but a short step.

The Catholic problem, especially after 1830, was equally obvious. Between 1830 and 1860 the number of Catholics in the United States grew from about 318,000 to over 3,100,000, an increase of some 900 percent. Where in 1830 Catholics had been less than 3 percent of the population, in 1860 they were about 10 percent. Most of the increase had come from immigration. As the number of immigrants steadily mounted (in the 1830s the annual average was some 60,000, while in the 1850s it was close to 250,-000), American nativists could *see* them everywhere: "crowding our cities," wrote one worried observer, "lining our railroads and canals . . . and *electing our rulers*." The problem was now neither remote nor theoretical. It was present and pressing. Anti-Catholics and nativists generally, both moderate and extreme, had to look to their laurels. Once the modern temperance and nativist crusades had begun, it was certain that their warriors would vastly outnumber those in the ranks of utopian radicalism. In the 1850s they were to be counted in the hundreds of thousands; those of the utopian radicals were to be counted merely in the hundreds, and they were very much divided in their objectives.

When trying to determine the consequences of reform for the American people, however, the historian had to do something more than count noses—and something more, too, than try to measure the distances between objectives and accomplishments. To do such things was to assess some of the social consequences of antebellum reform, but to do nothing more than count or measure was to ignore reform's consequences for individual participants. To point out, for example, that the numerical strength of each of the dozens of small religious sects in the United States—like the Mormons, the Millerites, and the Shakers, or the Rappites, the Zoarites, the Bethelites, and even the Two-Seed-in-the-Spirit Predestinarian Baptists—never matched the strength of the Methodists, the orthodox Baptists, or the various Presbyterian groups was to ignore the small sects' importance for their individual members. To point out that Dorothea Dix and a few coworkers induced more than a dozen state legislatures to pass laws to improve the institutional care of the insane by 1860 was to ignore the consequences of reform for Miss Dix personally and for the wretches she helped. By 1860, again, many states had responded to pleas and arguments for women's rights by passing laws permitting married women to own and control property. If such laws were important, noting them—or noting that an occasional woman like Elizabeth Blackwell in medicine or Antoinette Brown in the ministry entered fields hitherto reserved to men—said nothing about what the women's rights crusade meant emotionally and intellectually to individual crusaders. Nor was either the size or the enthusiasm of religious revival audiences, or even the number of converts, a measure of the impact of any preacher upon his individual listeners in the years after the preacher left town.

The difficulties of measuring such individual consequences of reform are obviously enormous. The large majority of the reformers—the followers and the converts, that is, rather than the leaders—left no evidence of what reform meant to them, or exactly why they followed one pied piper rather than another. Once more taking the antebellum reform movements together, they offered satisfactions for every human need and emotion. The historian can assume that somewhere, sometime, all the needs and emotions he can identify as characteristic of human beings were satisfied: love and hate, altruism and egotism, a yearning for the new and a desire for the old, a longing for persecution and a longing for God's grace, an eagerness for secular happiness and an eagerness to escape from a sorrowful and ungodly world, monogamous urgings and polygamous lusts, and many more. But no historian could say which motive was operative for a given man at a given time. Any reform movement could satisfy different needs together. Was it more a desire to do God's will or more a desire to preserve social stability that motivated the leaders and members of the national moral reform societies? Was it benevolence or was it a desire to observe and savor filth and corruption directly that drove on Dorothea Dix and her followers? Historians have long accepted the thesis of H. Richard Niebuhr's great work, *The Social Sources of Denominationalism* (New York, 1929), that the appeal of new religious cults and sects in Europe and America alike was to the socially dispossessed, the lower classes generally. Through unusual rites and novel creeds they sought religions more satisfactory than the traditional, conservative, rigid religions of men more powerful and more respectable. Yet in antebellum America it was clear that many downtrodden men sought solace not only in such sects as Universalism, Millerism, Mormonism, or the more enthusiastic varieties of Methodism and Presbyterianism, but also in the more respectable churches as well. Wherein lay the different beliefs and different memberships? Timothy L. Smith demonstrated in his *Revivalism and Social Reform in Mid-Nineteenth-Century America* that revivalism was popular not only in the nation's rural and western areas, as so many historians have pointed out, but in the urban centers of both West and East. If enthusiastic religion satisfied the peculiar needs of men on the frontier, it also satisfied the needs of city folk. Environment was less important than men's emotions in directing their search for excitement, for peace of soul, and for God Himself.

The ferment of antebellum reform, then, was an outpouring not only of humanitarianism, or Christian love, or a desire to realize fully the principles of American democracy. Reform was also an outpouring of all the peculiar aspects of human nature in antebellum America. Through reform, as it were, the historian could see Americans at their best and Americans at their worst, Americans at the heights of samaritanism and Americans at the depths of pharisaism, and Americans everywhere in between. Reform itself was among the most significant activities of the pre-Civil War years. But its significance lay not merely in its social consequences or in the fact that reform manifested a present freedom and a hope of greater freedom and happiness in the future. Its importance lay also in showing the varieties of mind and emotion that existed in a diverse nation of diverse persons, each of those persons unique, each of them striving in a way uniquely his own to satisfy the peculiar cravings of his heart and the peculiar urgings of his mind.

Every reform, in short, was important when some men, however few they were, thought it important. Yet when social significance was combined with the varieties of individual satisfaction, it was apparent that the different forms of antislaveryism and anti-southernism as they appeared in the years between 1854 and 1860 proved more significant than other reforms in shaping the nation's destiny. By 1860 and 1861 those movements in combination, with the Republican party as their bond of union, had not yet carried the day. It was clear, however, that in the Republican party itself and in the determination of most northerners to crush southern secession, antebellum reform reached its zenith of ferment and national importance.

Like other political organizations, the Republican party was a curious amalgam of different ideas and different men. Unfortunately a full account of the party's formative years still awaits the labors of some diligent historian willing to suffer much for the sake of enlightenment. But there are many valuable general works, limited studies, and biographies such as Allan Nevins's *Ordeal of the Union* and *The Emergence of Lincoln* (2 vols., New York, 1950); Andrew W. Crandall's *The Early History of the Republican*

Party, 1854-1856 (Boston, 1930); David M. Potter's *Lincoln and His Party in the Secession Crisis* (New Haven, 1942); Benjamin P. Thomas's *Abraham Lincoln* (New York, 1954); David Donald's *Charles Sumner and the Coming of the Civil War* (New York, 1960); and Hans L. Trefousse's *Benjamin Franklin Wade: Radical Senator from Ohio* (New York, 1963). These and other works make it plain that men joined the new party for a host of reasons: to increase their political power, to promote the causes of internal improvements and free homesteads at government expense, to get higher tariffs for American industrialists, to find a new political home now that the Whig party was dying and the Democratic party was wrangling and dividing over the slavery question. Yet the great principle for which the Republican party stood, the strongest plank in its platform—even if some Republican voters did not much admire its grainy, rough-hewn texture—was opposition to the expansion of slavery into territories originally closed to it by the Missouri Compromise of 1820. The Kansas-Nebraska Act had repealed that essential part of the Compromise, and the Republican party's strongest foundation was the resulting northern wrath.

A century later the reasons for the great northern anger were still not entirely clear. Until 1854 most northerners had been unwilling to join any movement to restrict the further spread of slavery. Since the 1830s, as Gilbert H. Barnes's *The Antislavery Impulse,* Dwight L. Dumond's *Antislavery,* and many other works had emphasized, abolitionists had been urging Congress to contain slavery in the states where it then existed. Believing that restricting slavery would help to destroy it—though the relation between means and ends was always obscure—abolitionists of a political bent had demanded cooperation from national politicians. Failing to get it in adequate amounts, they had organized first the Liberty party in 1840 and then the Free Soil party in 1848. But abolition leaders such as James G. Birney, Salmon P. Chase, and Joshua Giddings of Ohio, George W. Julian of Indiana, and John P. Hale of New

Hampshire had discovered that the Liberty and Free Soil parties had no appeal for most present Whigs and Democrats. It was certain that both of the older parties contained men who disliked both slavery and the slaveholders' political power. Antislavery Whigs and Democrats alike, for example, had supported the Wilmot Proviso in 1846—though David C. Wilmot himself was no abolitionist—and Congress and conventions of both parties had been arguing the morality of slavery for years. But until 1854 the come-outer spirit in the two parties was weak indeed.

By that time, however, the political situation was much different than it had been just a few years earlier—at the time of the Compromise of 1850, say, or of the national elections of 1852. For one thing, even before the passage of the Kansas-Nebraska Act Whigs and Democrats and Free Soilers had begun cooperating in so-called "fusion" movements in the northern states. The fusionists' principles were distinctly reformist. Men who would become Republicans in the near future were slowly gathering prohibitionists, nativists, and antislaveryites into new organizations, building new structures on a long-standing foundation of moral reform. Most of the fusionists were Whigs, who saw only a dark future for their party after their defeats in 1852—the Whig party now seemed likely to become a permanent minority—and who had themselves a tendency toward reform of one kind or another. Like-minded Democrats, especially antislaveryites and men who were unhappy with the power of southerners within the party, joined their former enemies. Thus when passage of the Kansas-Nebraska Act appeared certain, and then occurred, proto-Republican parties already existed in the northern states, and their leaders had no difficulty adding anti-Nebraskaism to their platforms.

But none of this explained why northerners disliked the Kansas-Nebraska Act so much, why they flocked into the Republican party in such large numbers. It was not the practical desires of politicians, after all, nor their personal dislike of slavery, either, that was responsible for the appearance and growth of

Republicanism. Instead, it was the support of the people for the ideas that politicians offered. From 1854 to 1856, moreover, those ideas had increasingly to do with southern slavery and its expansion into Kansas Territory, at the expense of prohibition and nativism. Andrew W. Crandall's *The Early History of the Republican Party* and C. S. Griffin's *Their Brothers' Keepers* have noted that after 1854 and 1855 the Republican fusionists in most northern states found that the varieties of antislaveryism and antisouthernism were far more popular vote-getters. The reasons for the declining attractiveness of prohibitionism to many Republican leaders were easy to see. A moralist such as Neal Dow in Maine, who became one of the more active Republicans, intended to champion Maine Laws forever, whatever the political consequences. But men less committed than he knew that Republicanism had to appeal to the wets as well as the drys to be successful. When the lure of anti-Nebraskaism proved more popular than the lure of prohibitionism, Republican leaders quieted their temperance enthusiasm, and then stilled it altogether. Dow himself helped to wreck his own cause. After the Maine legislature of 1855 had passed a more stringent prohibition law, an anti-Dow mob gathered in the streets of Portland and then attacked a legal liquor store in the city hall, which held spirits for sale for the permitted medicinal and industrial uses. At the time Dow was mayor of Portland. At the height of the riot he ordered city militiamen to fire into the mob. They killed one man and wounded seven others. This irresponsible and foolish act and the hatred of Dow that it inspired so alarmed the state's Republican leaders that in 1856 they refused to endorse the Maine Law in the party platform.

Nativism also declined in 1855 and 1856, but for more complex reasons. In the mid-1850s nativism fed itself in peculiar ways on party discord and sectional antagonism. While many early Republicans in the North used it to improve their political fortunes, other northerners and many southerners saw it as a means of restoring sectional harmony. Some politicians believed that if native-born Americans could concentrate their hatred on foreigners generally and Roman Catholics in particular, they could, perhaps, forget their hatred for each other. In that spirit Kenneth Raynor of North Carolina proposed at the meeting of the National Council of the Order of the Star-Spangled Banner in 1854 that it create a Union degree in the Order's lodges. The degree would bind every man taking it to "discourage and denounce any attempt coming from any quarter . . . to destroy or subvert" the Union and to vote only for nationalists. The National Council approved Raynor's proposal, and within six months 1,500,000 members had taken the new degree. But at the same time, by contrast, the abolitionist Salmon P. Chase was suggesting that anti-Nebraska men should indulge themselves in more opposition to "papal influence" and "organized foreignism" for the sake of votes, and abolitionists such as Henry Wilson of Massachusetts were joining the Order itself. A national party that tried to include antislaveryites, proslaveryites, and men who wished only to dissolve the growing sectionalism could not long stand. In June, 1855, the National Council adopted a proslavery report stating that Congress should not legislate on the subject of slavery in the territories, whereupon Henry Wilson and his group of northern antislaveryites walked out. Wilson returned to Massachusetts determined to blast the Know-Nothing party to "hell and damnation," and there were now North Americans and South Americans.

In addition to the division caused by the slavery argument, the Know-Nothing party suffered other calamities. The state legislatures dominated by Know-Nothings proved incapable of enacting anti-Catholic, anti-immigrant laws. The rise of Know-Nothingism stimulated a powerful opposition. Opponents heaped ridicule on the Order's principles and its secret rituals, and when Know-Nothings and their allies in several cities used violence against the foreign-born, the immigrants struck back just as violently. There were riots and killings in Baltimore, New Orleans, St. Louis, Louisville, and other cities. Still more, the Know-Nothings suffered from their inability to agree on basic ideas. In the Southwest, for example, especially in Louisiana, Roman Catholics from older families had joined the party to protest the immigration of Irishmen and Germans. In the Northwest many Know-Nothing leaders professed their friendship for immigrants in general, but took a strong stand against Catholicism. Beset on all sides by apparently insoluble problems, by the presidential elections of 1856 the Know-Nothing party was mainly a Unionist party dedicated to protecting the nation from antislavery and proslavery extremists. Its candidate for President was ex-President Millard Fillmore of New York. Fillmore was a devoted Unionist, but—as Robert J. Rayback has shown in an excellent biography, *Millard Fillmore: Biography of a President* (Buffalo, 1959)—he was no dedicated nativist.

By late 1856, then, Republican leaders believed nativism a liability rather than an asset; and the more they thought about the votes that immigrants had, the less they espoused nativist ideas. Self-shorn of prohibitionism and nativism, the Republican party stood mainly and clearly on the principle of opposing the expansion of slavery into the territories. Whether that stand made the Republican party an abolition party, however, was not so clear. Was the party's goal merely to prevent slavery's growth and repeal the Kansas-Nebraska Act, or was it to strike a blow at slavery in the states where it existed? Answering that most important question involved difficulties of several kinds. The first was defining the words "abolition" and "abolitionist." Larry Gara's perceptive article "Who Was an Abolitionist?" in Martin B. Duberman, ed., *The Antislavery Vanguard: New Essays on the Abolitionists* (Princeton, 1965), showed that even the men of the time could not agree on who was an abolitionist and who was not. There were Garrisonian abolitionists and anti-Garrisonian abolitionists— but to the Garrisonians the anti-Garrisonians were not abolitionists at all. There were abolitionists who favored social equality for freed Negroes and abolitionists who detested Negroes, and the former called the latter traitors to abolitionism. If some abolitionists from the 1830s on hoped that preventing slavery's expansion would weaken the peculiar institution in the states where it already existed, many men who fought slavery's expansion—such as David C. Wilmot of Wilmot Proviso fame—denied that they were abolitionists. "There has already arisen so many various [abolition] sects . . . ," said one astute observer in 1844, "that the term 'abolition' like the term 'orthodox' really means that a man may believe 'some things as well as others,' provided he sticks hard to the name." Historians, Gara urged, should use the words "abolition" and "abolitionist" with the utmost caution and should make careful distinctions in applying them to men and groups.

Gara's point was well taken, especially as it applied to the Republicans. The party platform of 1856 heatedly opposed the expansion of slavery into the territories and described slavery itself as one of the "twin relics of barbarism"—Mormon polygamy was the other. But the platform said nothing about interfering with slavery in the states where it existed. The platform of 1860 denounced slavery in the territories and the African slave trade, which abolitionists of every hue had been fighting for years. Yet the platform also said that each state had the right to control "its own domestic institutions according to its own judgment exclusively"; that right was "essential to that balance of powers on which the perfection and endurance of our political fabric" depended. If the Republican party included ardent antislaveryites—such as Joshua Giddings, Salmon P. Chase, and Charles Sumner—who had long fought slavery and were doing all they could to hasten its abolition, it also included moderates and conservatives such as Thurlow Weed of New York, Simon Cameron of Pennsylvania, and Edward Bates of Missouri. The moderates were willing enough to see slavery's expansion checked, but wholly unwilling to attack southern slavery violently, either by word or deed.

The Republican party, it seemed, could be all things to all northerners. But to the greatest Republican of them all, the party *was* an abolition party, if "abolition" be given a broad definition. Abraham Lincoln had detested slavery for years before his rise to national prominence in the late 1850s. In his eyes the Republican party was a means of making the wrong of slavery manifest and of ending the wrong. "The real issue in this controversy—the one pressing upon every mind—" Lincoln said in his last debate with Stephen A. Douglas in 1858, "is the sentiment on the part of one class that looks upon the institution of slavery *as a wrong,* and of another class that *does not* look upon it as a wrong. The sentiment that contemplates the institution of slavery in this country as a wrong is the sentiment of the Republican party. It is the sentiment around which all their actions—all their arguments circle—from which all their propositions radiate." Republicans, Lincoln said, saw slavery "as being a moral, social and political wrong"; they insisted that it be treated as a wrong. One of the means of so treating it was to make provision that it grow no larger. But Republicans, Lincoln said, "also desire a policy that looks to a peaceful end of slavery at sometime, as being wrong." Lincoln's consistent position was that the American people should place slavery "in the course of ultimate extinction," or where the "public mind rested in the belief that it *was* in the course of ultimate extinction." Both in the debates with Douglas and in many later speeches Lincoln labored mightily to convince present and prospective Republican voters that this was where the Founding Fathers had placed it, and that his generation of Americans should follow the Fathers' example. "I have no doubt," he said on September 15, 1858, at Jonesboro, Illinois, in the third debate with Douglas, "that it *would* become extinct, for all time to come, if we but re-adopted the policy of the fathers by restricting it to the limits it has already covered—restricting it from the new Territories."

Now if an abolitionist be defined only as a Garrisonian or Wendell Phillipsite fanatic, only as a man who attacked slavery and slaveholders vengefully, viciously, and splenetically, Lincoln was no abolitionist. "Lincoln was far from being an abolitionist" in his run for the Senate in 1858, James G. Randall wrote in his *Lincoln the President* (4 vols., New York, 1945-1955). Nothing, Randall wrote, was "more obvious in the controlling counsels of Lincoln's party in that period than the avoidance of any 'ultra'— i.e., strongly abolitionist—tone. The 'peculiar institution' was not being assailed by the Republican party in the commonwealths where it existed," by which Randall meant that it was not being assailed as Garrison, Joshua Giddings, or Charles Sumner assailed it. But if an abolitionist be defined as a man who disliked slavery, who desired its end—even if that end was to come far in the future—and who acted toward that end, Lincoln and the Republicans for whom he spoke were certainly abolitionists; and southerners properly identified them as such.

By that definition the Republican party—or at least the part that Lincoln led, together with the group of more virulent abolitionists who stood to his left—was the climax of antebellum reform. It was alike the most important manifestation and the most important outgrowth of the reforming spirit. Yet by the early months of 1861 the southern response to Lincoln's election and to the party's other successes at the northern polls had called forth a reform movement far more significant for American history, for the Americans of the present and future generations, than any movement of the antebellum years. In the eyes of most northern reformers, southern secession was the greatest evil, the greatest threat to happiness, freedom, political democracy, natural rights, human progress, and the will of God that the nation had faced. The reformers who sought to preserve the Union did so in the name of all the principles in whose behalf reformers had claimed to act during the preceding three decades. But in the war against the southern states would also appear all those other less attractive attributes of antebellum reformers: hatred, a vengeful spirit, a meanness of mind, an inability or an unwillingness to see virtue in other men's ideas and other ways of life.

LOOKING BACKWARD

When the American people and their historians of later generations looked back on antebellum reform, they saw in it what they wished to see. The temperance men and women's-righters of the post-Civil War years, for example, would continue to be inspired by what they and their predecessors had done. Postwar nativists and prison reformers and religious revivalists and communitarian socialists and reformers of several dozen other kinds would find inspiration in the beginnings and accomplishments of the antebellum years. Historians who followed the lead of Arthur M. Schlesinger, Sr., and Alice Felt Tyler would try to pass on to their readers the faith in American democracy and all the other good things that had allegedly infused and inspired the reformers' work. In the 1960s, when many Americans were seeking equal rights of several different kinds for Negroes, they and the historians who spoke for them strove to raise the antebellum abolitionists from the low places into which they felt that other, less sympathetic historians had cast them. Attacking the antiabolitionism of many historians, Martin B. Duberman's "The Northern Response to Slavery," in *The Antislavery Vanguard*—the title was surely meant to designate the authors who wrote the so-called "new essays" on the abolitionists as well as the men of whom they wrote—eagerly defended the antebellum zealots. "Surely there is now evidence enough to suggest that commitment and concern need not be aberrations; they may represent the profoundest elements of our humanity," Duberman wrote. "Surely there are grounds for believing that those who protested strongly against slavery were not all misguided fanatics or frustrated neurotics—though by so believing it becomes easier to ignore the injustices against which they protested. Perhaps it is time to ask whether the abolitionists, in insisting that slavery be ended, were indeed those men of their generation furthest removed from reality, or whether that description should be reserved for those Northerners who remained indifferent to the institution, and those Southerners who defended it as a 'positive good.' From the point of view of these men, the abolitionists were indeed mad, but it is time we questioned the sanity of the point of view." Not enough modern historians were defending the abolitionists, Fawn M. Brodie said in an essay, "Who Defends the Abolitionist?" in the same volume. Howard Zinn's "Abolitionists, Freedom-Riders, and the Tactics of Agitation," also in *The Antislavery Vanguard,* said bluntly that "scholarly detachment from the profound ethical conflicts of society" and from "human concern"—that is, from concern about the evil of slavery and the necessity of its abolition—made scholarship merely a "pretentious game."

To understand both the abolitionists and the other antebellum reformers, however, did not require the student of history to project his own prejudices backward in time. A hundred years after the Civil War the question of whether the reformers were right or wrong, good or bad, defensible or indefensible, could matter only to contemporary moralists and preachers. An understanding of the reformers required an openness of mind, a willingness *not* to care whether they served America well or served America ill. It required in addition only a desire to study a group of intrinsically fascinating people for the sake of the delights of meeting them and a desire to discover why so many Americans joined in one of the most intimate and personal activities known to man: making others perceive and behave according to one's own ideas. Satisfying such desires was an activity worthy enough in its own right.

But a knowledge of the antebellum reformers could have a utilitarian as well as an intrinsic value. A century after the Civil War there was a new ferment of reform abroad in the United States. It embraced, as did the reform movement of old, an enormous variety of ideals: pacifism, anarchism, and Christian ecumenicalism; civil rights, black power, and student power; sexual freedom, psychedelic satisfactions, and the replacement of the reign of force by the reign of love; and many more. The modern reformers—and, indeed, everyone who "espouses for the time the cause of man"—could gain greater self-knowledge, with its intermingled pleasures and pains, by meeting across the years men and women of their own kind.

Bibliographical Essay

Because no historian has yet dealt fully with Ralph Waldo Emerson's shrewd ideas about the natures of reform and reformers, the student should try to do so before reading the historians' works. In the light of Emerson's thoughts about the relations between reform and conservatism and about the peculiar differences between the quality of reform and the quality of the reformers' activities, both the strengths and the weaknesses of the secondary accounts become clearer. Emerson's ideas are in three essays, all of which are esthetically charming as well as intellectually stimulating: "Man the Reformer," "Lecture on the Times," and "The Conservative," in Ralph Waldo Emerson, *Nature, Addresses, and Lectures,* ed. Edward Waldo Emerson (Boston, 1903). Emerson's sympathy with the general idea of reform makes the sympathy of most historians easier to understand; his criticisms of the reformers in action make more intelligible both the lack of such criticism in so many accounts of antebellum reform and the critical remarks that a minority of historians have made.

Although a reader with Emersonian proclivities—which, obviously, I have—will find fault with much of the secondary literature on antebellum reform, in that literature there is much of value. If only because Arthur M. Schlesinger, Sr.'s *The American as Reformer* (Cambridge, 1951) is the one work of its kind, it possesses a peculiar merit. In attempting to view American reform whole, Schlesinger made the antebellum reformers part of a continuing tradition in the nation's history, both as they drew upon the past and as they helped to shape the future. The book is marred, however, by Schlesinger's uncritical praise of the men he sees as reformers, by his simplifications of their motives and objectives, and by his desire to instill in his readers a deeper appreciation of the so-called "liberal" reforms of his own day. Alice Felt Tyler's *Freedom's Ferment: Phases of American Social History to 1860* (Minneapolis, 1944) suffers from the same deficiencies, although her book is less concerned than Schlesinger's with contemporary events. *Freedom's Ferment* provides an excellent synthesis of the earlier writings on those antebellum Americans whom most historians consider reformers, and its style is sprightly. In addition to its information, *Freedom's Ferment* has a splendid bibliography of earlier writings. A less satisfactory general work than Mrs. Tyler's, but one that still bears careful reading, is Russel B. Nye's *William Lloyd Garrison and the Humanitarian Reformers* (Boston, 1955). The book says more about the abolitionists than about other humanitarians, and it is often superficial. Yet it remains a good general introduction to the era of reform.

Before starting to read the specialized monographs and biographies about antebellum reform, the student should investigate several books that describe the intellectual and social environment in which the reformers labored. Although Vernon L. Parrington's *The Romantic Revolution in America, 1800-1860*—the second volume of his *Main Currents in American Thought: An Interpretation of American Literature from the Beginnings to 1920* (3 vols., New York, 1927-30)—is fearfully prejudiced in favor of Jeffersonian "liberalism" and badly outdated as well, it still bears careful scrutiny and provides delightful reading. Arthur A. Ekirch's *The Idea of Progress in America, 1815-1860* (New York, 1944) offers a multitude of shrewd insights and contemporary quotations in demonstrating how firmly most Americans believed that progress in the United States was inevitable. The study of nineteenth-century American nationalism, which both spurred the reformers to action and which the reformers so much encouraged, is still, inexplicably and incredibly, in a rudimentary stage. But Hans Kohn's *American Nationalism: An Interpretative Essay* (New York, 1957) analyzes the elements of nationalistic ideas that appeared in the thought of many of the country's prominent men, and Paul C. Nagel's *One Nation Indivisible: The Union in American Thought, 1776-1861* (New York, 1964), though unsystematic, disjointed, and impressionistic, helps to explain why the idea of union proved so compelling to nineteenth-century Americans. George M. Fredrickson's *The Inner Civil War: Northern Intellectuals and the Crisis of the Union* (New York, 1965) portrays satisfactorily the varied reactions of selected northern writers and thinkers, including many antebellum reformers, to the nation dividing, divided, and reconstructed. Because the varieties of American romanticism so infused the ferment of antebellum reform, the student should have the pleasant experience of reading F. O. Matthiessen, *American Renaissance: Art and Expression in the Age of Emerson and Whitman* (New York, 1941), which is intellectual history at its best. Rollin G. Osterweis, *Romanticism and Nationalism in the Old South* (New Haven, 1949) shows that southerners shared the same spirit that stimulated so many northerners, although that spirit took very different forms below the Mason-Dixon line. Because the distinction between what historians call "reform" and other kinds of antebellum activity is still vague, the student should investigate the nature and meaning of Jacksonian Democracy. A convenient introduction to that controversial subject is John William Ward's "The Age of the Common Man," in John Higham, ed., *The Reconstruction of American History* (New York, 1962), pp. 82-97. Since every explanation of the origins of the Civil War must deal with the reform spirit in general and the antislavery crusade in particular, the student should plunge into the swirl of argument about the war's causes through Thomas J. Pressly's *Americans Interpret Their Civil War* (Princeton, 1954). A masterly synthesis of the nation's history from the mid-1840s on is Allan Nevins's *Ordeal of the Union* (2 vols., New York, 1947) and *The Emergence of Lincoln* (2 vols., New York, 1950). Both works are pro-Unionist and antislavery, yet both are sensitive and sympathetic to the nuances of the many problems that men of all kinds in all sections had to face.

The abolitionists, certainly the most important of the antebellum reformers, should be studied before the others. Although there is still no completely satisfactory account of the whole antislavery movement, Louis Filler's *The Crusade against Slavery, 1830-1860* (New York, 1960) and Dwight L. Dumond's *Antislavery: The Crusade for Freedom in America* (Ann Arbor, 1961) demand careful, thoughtful reading. Both Filler and Dumond are latter-day antislaveryites who

condemn slavery and approve abolitionism. Both books suffer from
their authors' prejudices—especially Dumond's, which frequently
degenerates into an antislavery screed. Once their easily recognized
prejudices are dismissed, however, residues of good history remain.
Along with most other recent historians of abolitionism, Filler and
Dumond learned much about antislaveryism outside New England
and about the relation between moral antislaveryism and political action from Gilbert H. Barnes's *The Antislavery Impulse, 1830-1844*
(New York, 1933). That work not only began a controversy about
the origins of the antislavery movement after 1830, but saw a close
relation between abolitionism in the middle states and the moral reforms of the great national benevolent societies, centered in New
York City. Barnes was so obsessed with both the western origins of
abolitionism and the structure of what he called the "benevolent empire" of moral reform societies that he bent his evidence to the break-
ing point; it simply would not prove what he wanted it to prove. Both
C. S. Griffin's *Their Brothers' Keepers: Moral Stewardship in the
United States, 1800-1865* (New Brunswick, 1960) and Charles I.
Foster's *An Errand of Mercy: The Evangelical United Front, 1790-
1837* (Chapel Hill, 1960) are superior to *The Antislavery Impulse*
in describing the nature and workings of the reform societies and
disprove Barnes's idea that in the 1830s there existed a benevolent empire with so-called "interlocking directorates" of reformers. The ideas
and activity of one of Barnes's chief protagonists appear in Benjamin
P. Thomas, *Theodore Weld: Crusader for Freedom* (New Brunswick,
1950), which is both perceptive and sympathetic. But to understand
just how far Barnes and Dumond and other champions of the western
antislaveryites missed the mark of truth, John L. Thomas's *The
Liberator: William Lloyd Garrison, A Biography* (Boston, 1963),
Walter M. Merrill's *Against Wind and Tide: A Biography of Wm.
Lloyd Garrison* (Cambridge, 1963), and Irving H. Bartlett's *Wendell
Phillips: Brahmin Radical* (Boston, 1961) are indispensable. Thomas's
biography is the best of the three; it is a powerful, irreverent, and
thorough study of the most complex and compelling of all the reformers. For a better appreciation of the various forms that antislaveryism took, Philip J. Staudenraus's excellent *The African Colonization Movement, 1816-1865* (New York, 1961) is required reading.
    After reading these works and thereby gaining a familiarity with
the antislaveryites, many students may wish to work their way through
the studied complexities of Stanley M. Elkins, *Slavery: A Problem*

in American Institutional and Intellectual Life (Chicago, 1959). Like other historians who hope that the insights of psychologists and sociologists will give their history greater meaning and sophistication, Elkins makes great generalizations about abolitionists on the basis of limited and routine evidence. Yet Elkins sees and stresses a most important point: that of all the pre-Civil War reformers the northern abolitionists were the farthest removed, both personally and institutionally, from the evils they fought. That separation between them and slavery, Elkins believes, made them irresponsible in their condemnation of slavery and southerners, and caused them to indulge in moral censure at the expense of efforts to devise reasonable and workable plans for abolition. For several perceptive articles on various aspects of antislaveryism, one should see Martin B. Duberman, ed., *The Antislavery Vanguard: New Essays on the Abolitionists* (Princeton, 1965). But beware. While several of the articles—David Brion Davis's "Slavery and Sin: The Cultural Background," for example, or John L. Thomas's "Antislavery and Utopia"—are very good indeed, others —such as Fawn M. Brodie's "Who Defends the Abolitionist?" or Silvan S. Tompkins's "The Psychology of Commitment: The Constructive Role of Violence and Suffering for the Individual and for His Society"—are merely preachily impassioned or pseudosophisticated restatements of familiar material.

Most of the other antebellum reformers have not generated such controversy as have the abolitionists. To be sure, in some areas of reform there is continuing argument. In the women's rights movement, for example, the traditional pieties expressed in such works as Otelia Cromwell's *Lucretia Mott* (Cambridge, 1958) or Elinor Rice Hays's *Morning Star: A Biography of Lucy Stone, 1818-1893* (New York, 1961) receive severe challenge in Robert E. Riegel's *American Feminists* (Lawrence, 1963), whose ideas are neither traditional nor pious. Riegel's book, however, suffers from an oft-considerable want of evidence for its oft-agreeable generalizations. But more common than the controversial works about reformers are the monographs that most historians accept as at least standard, if not absolutely definitive, accounts—if only because no work has appeared to replace or contradict them. Thus Merle E. Curti's *The American Peace Crusade, 1815-1860* (Durham, 1929) is the standard work on antebellum pacifism and John A. Krout's *The Origins of Prohibition* (New York, 1925) is the standard history of the temperance movement until the passage of the Maine Law. More recently, however,

Frank L. Byrne published an excellent study of the *Prophet of Prohibition: Neal Dow and His Crusade* (Madison, 1961), which probes the ideas, emotions, and activities of the greatest prewar temperance leader far more deeply than Krout did for any of his cold-water advocates. On the reformers who believed that institutionalized education was a cure for the country's ills and a preserver of its virtues—no reputable historian has disagreed with them—Louise Hall Thorp's *Until Victory: Horace Mann and Mary Peabody* (Boston, 1953), Carl Bode's *The American Lyceum: Town Meeting of the Mind* (New York, 1956), and the early sections of Frederick Rudolph's *The American College and University: A History* (New York, 1962) are informative and well written. Blake McKelvey's *American Prisons: A Study in American Social History Prior to 1915* (Chicago, 1936) remains the best general account of the nation's jails and their reformers; but W. David Lewis's *From Newgate to Dannemora: The Rise of the Penitentiary in New York, 1796-1848* (Ithaca, 1965) is deeper in insight and more thorough in research for developments in the all-important Empire State. Two standard biographies of reformers who, for reasons both egotistic and altruistic, tried to improve the ways in which society cared for its rejects are Helen E. Marshall's *Dorothea Dix, Forgotten Samaritan* (Chapel Hill, 1937) and Harold Schwartz's *Samuel Gridley Howe: Social Reformer, 1801-1876* (Cambridge, 1956). The study of antebellum attitudes toward poverty is still incomplete, but Robert H. Bremner's *From the Depths: The Discovery of Poverty in the United States* (New York, 1956) has much information presented with as much objectivity as Bremner's compassion permits. To perceive how a movement that many historians take to be laughable quackery actually manifested an honest desire to learn more about the laws of human behavior, see John D. Davies, *Phrenology, Fad and Science: A Nineteenth Century American Crusade* (New Haven, 1955). And on the labor movement the interested student will wish to read the relevant parts of Foster R. Dulles's *Labor in America: A History* (2d ed., New York, 1960).

After sampling even this limited selection of the hundreds of monographs on antebellum reform and reformers, the student will be better able to appreciate the variety and contrariness of the reform ferment. Rather than despair at the want of unifying themes, however, he should increase his perplexity the more, for until the diversity and the contradictions are fully explored, reform cannot be understood. One excellent way to grasp the pluralism of American life is to study the Americans' ideas about God and the practices to which those ideas led. Whitney R. Cross's *The Burned-Over District: The Social and Intellectual History of Enthusiastic Religion in Western New York, 1800-1850* (Ithaca, 1950) and Book One of Perry Miller's *The Life of the Mind in America: From the Revolution to the Civil War* (New York, 1965) are excellent accounts of antebellum evangelicalism and its social significance. To appreciate the diversity of American religious experience, the student ought to compare Bernard A. Weisberger's lively *They Gathered at the River: The Story of the Great Revivalists and Their Impact upon Religion in America* (Boston, 1958) with Octavius B. Frothingham's still valuable study—and appreciation—of *Transcendentalism in New England* (New York, 1876). Moving off on a tangent to both evangelicalism and transcendentalism, the reader can join Fawn M. Brodie's critical tour through the personality of Joseph Smith in *No Man Knows My History: The Life of Joseph Smith, the Mormon Prophet* (New York, 1945), and then join John Humphrey Noyes on a perceptive journey through his own spirit in G. N. Noyes, ed., *The Religious Experiences of John Humphrey Noyes* (New York, 1923). The curious ideas and practices of still another group are set forth lucidly in Edward D. Andrews, *The People Called Shakers: A Search for the Perfect Society* (New York, 1953), while Clara Sears's *Days of Delusion* (Boston, 1924) tells of the Millerites, perhaps the strangest religious group—indeed, perhaps the strangest reform group—of them all.

INDEX